D0385392

The Little Book
of

CELTIC MYTHS
& LEGENDS

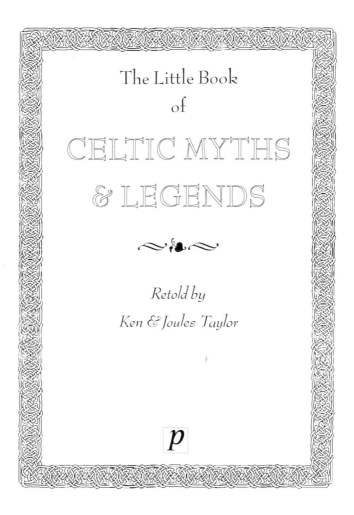

The Little Book
of

CELTIC MYTHS
& LEGENDS

Retold by
Ken & Joules Taylor

p

This is a Parragon Book

This edition published in 2000

Parragon
Queen Street House
4 Queen Street
Bath BA1 1HE, UK

Produced by Magpie Books, an imprint of
Robinson Publishing Ltd, London

ISBN 0-75253-172-7

A copy of the British Library Cataloguing-in-
Publication Data is available from the British Library
Printed in China

Contents

∽

Introduction   7

∽ SCOTTISH ∽

Introduction

~

Like the Celts themselves, Celtic myths and legends are robust and colorful. This selection is drawn from Wales, Ireland and Scotland, and gives a taste of their wide variety of themes and styles.

The Celts chose not to entrust their ancestral tales to writing, preferring instead the intimate and entertaining tradition of verbal storytelling, often by professional bards.

This oral transmission allowed stories to develop over the years. Although retaining their ancient folk wisdom, they also maintained their relevance to the day-to-day lives of the audience. In this book we have tried to make them accessible, enjoyable and satisfying for our own generation.

The general absence of deities in these myths is particularly notable, and is due to two factors. Firstly, they were first written down by Christian scribes who deliberately played down the importance of the native gods and goddesses. Secondly, the Celts tended to see divinity in everything – both in the forces of nature and in the very plants, animals and stones that surround us. In this pantheistic approach to life there is no clear distinction between an object and its spiritual presence and power.

In Britain and Ireland toward the end of the nineteenth century an artistic and philosophical movement (the poet W.B. Yeats was an important proponent) rejected the rigid moral doctrine and mechanistic scientific dogma of the time, and embraced the Celtic world view.

This powerful, idealistic vision continues to inspire people to peer into the Celtic twilight and see a future that celebrates the native traditions of these ancient isles.

TALIESIN AND THE CALDRONS

~

Many catastrophes not only blight the lives of
those at the center of the disaster, but also those
who were little more than innocent victims. And
strangely, but according to the balance of the
universe, we sometimes find that one of those
innocent bystanders will receive blessings greater
even than the misfortune which initially threatened
their very lives.

One such example is given in the story of the
rise of Taliesin.

Ceridwen, wife of a gentleman called Tegid
Voel, was a queen among witches. Their house
stood on stilts in the middle of Lake Tegid in the
north part of Wales, and they had three children: a
son called Morvran; a daughter called Creirwy who

was the most beautiful maiden in the land; and Avagddu who was so ugly that his prospects looked very dim indeed.

Ceridwen's skill in the magic arts was equal to her maternal devotion, and she determined to brew a magical potion for her shockingly disfigured son. This potion would imbue him with prodigious mental abilities and knowledge of life's most profound mysteries, and also give him the inspiration to use them wisely.

She used all the wisdom she possessed to gather the potent herbs and other ingredients that together could produce her heart's desire. She spared no expense and mustered some items so rare and precious that they could never again be found.

On Lunasadh, the first of August, she was ready to begin mixing the incomparable brew. She set a caldron to sit over a fire and assigned an old, blind man called Morda to tend the flames so that the liquid was always kept boiling. Then she appointed a youth, Gwion, to stir the mixture incessantly and warned him to take the greatest pains never to let a single drop be lost over the caldron's rim.

Their duties were no easy ones however, for the brew had to boil continuously for a year and a day.

The long year ahead grew gradually shorter, and still Ceridwen gathered and piled in fresh supplies of the magical herbs, and chanted her incantations ceaselessly.

One day, toward the end of the allotted time, while Ceridwen was away seeking more fresh ingredients, three small drops of the seething liquid burst from a bubble in the heart of the caldron and splashed up onto Gwion's hand.

It was the work of a moment to thrust his hand into his mouth, suck off the hot drips and soothe the scalded skin.

His instinct, however, was his doom. Such was the nature of the sorcery that all the magical power of the brimming caldron was instantly lost, and the whole of its strength entered Gwion's body and rapidly filled his mind!

Ceridwen's Wrath

~

Gwion's dawning powers of magical awareness left him in no doubt that Ceridwen would be insane with fury when she discovered that her long toil for her disadvantaged son had been irretrievably ruined.

In fact, the remaining liquid was not only exhausted of its invaluable properties, but had become so toxic that it destroyed the caldron and poured over the fire. Plants withered as it poisoned the soil, and it spilled into a nearby stream, instantly killing not only the fish but all the livestock that drank therefrom.

Gwion fled!

Sensing calamity, Ceridwen appeared on the scene of sudden desolation – and smote Morda on the head with a stave with such ferocity that one of his blind eyes fell out onto his cheek.

But she knew it was Gwion who had dashed her hopes, and she raced off in the direction of his home.

Gwion saw her gaining on him, and when she was hard on his heels he found the power to transform himself into a hare, and he leaped from side to side, evading her every effort to catch him.

In a trice she transformed herself into a greyhound and turned him from his course.

He ran toward a river, and as he dove into its swirling waters he became a fish, but she became an otter-bitch and chased him underwater.

He leaped as a salmon out of the current and swiftly became a bird, but she became a hawk and flew closer and closer to him.

He dropped to the ground at a threshing floor and, changing again, hid among the grains of wheat, but she became a night-black hen and sought him out again.

When she found him this time there was

no escape, and she swallowed him whole in the twinkling of her eye!

The Discovery of Taliesin

Nine months after Ceridwen swallowed Gwion she bore a son that was sired of no man. She knew it was Gwion, and had planned to exact her final revenge when the child was newborn and helpless, but when she saw the baby's beauty she could not take its life.

Instead, she placed the sleeping babe in a good leather bag and cast it into the sea, utterly at the mercy of fortune.

On the coast, a little way north of Aberystwyth, was a salmon weir that yielded never less than one hundred pounds of fish when it was emptied on May Day each year. The owner of this abundant weir had a son, Elphin, who was of an age when he had a wife and was ready to rule his own lands. But Elphin was plagued with bad luck in his every enterprise.

This year the old man decided to give the proceeds of the May Day catch to Elphin, to provide funds for his future. When they scoured the weir, though, not a single fish could be found, and the weir-wardens muttered that the lad was sorely cursed indeed.

Then one of them spied Ceridwen's leather bag, snagged on one of the poles. The first thing they saw upon opening it was the pale gleam of a baby's forehead: "Taliesin!" cried the warden in surprise.

"Taliesin, then, shall be his name," said Elphin, for "Radiant Brow" is what Taliesin means.

Elphin's Folly

~

Although Elphin was dismayed at the unparalleled absence of fish, he gently settled the baby on his horse and rode home with great care.

Along the way he was astonished to hear a small voice advising him that despair would bring no advantage, and that instead of lamenting his lack of gain, he should be prudent with what he did already possess.

Elphin was amazed when he realized it was the child speaking to him and, thinking it might be some strange spirit and not a mortal at all, tremblingly asked for the child to explain itself.

Thereupon Taliesin told of his troubles working for Ceridwen, as Gwion, and of the bizarre journey he had endured.

Elphin gave the child to his wife to nurse,

and for thirteen years Elphin's fortune improved as Taliesin advised him on many important matters.

Then, at Yule, Elphin was invited to the court of the ruler of the region. Here it was traditional for praises to be sung both about the lord's achievements and about the peerless glory of himself and his retinue.

Although he might have stayed silent once the twenty-four professional bards had ended their profuse and elaborate eulogies, Elphin felt impelled to speak. He quietly but very clearly proclaimed that, in all honesty, he reckoned himself favored with a wife entirely as virtuous as any lady in the kingdom. And, furthermore, he also had a bard as skilled as the best of the king's own bards.

This frank confession of Elphin's delight in his own good fortune was mistaken by the king for a direct challenge to his own sovereign superiority.

Almost before he knew what was happening, Elphin was dragged from the assembly, marched into a strong, cold prison in a high tower, and his feet secured with a thick chain. It seemed scant consolation that, because he was of royal blood, the chain was wrought from silver.

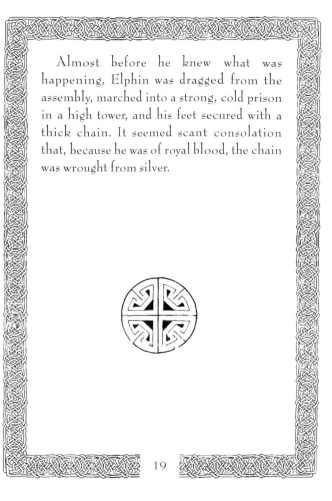

The Finger Ring

~

In order to test Elphin's claims, the king despatched his son to seduce the virtuous wife.

This young man had made many conquests of passion and was secretly feared by many maidens; his talents in this direction were legendary.

When he arrived and was admitted to meet the lady he found her richly attired and bedecked with many a gleaming jewel and valuable ring.

They dined together and, by the end of the evening, the woman was thoroughly intoxicated and the prince was convinced of her lack of virtue. As proof of her intemperance, he took out his knife and cut off her little finger at the knuckle.

Arriving back at court, the prince proudly displayed the grisly trophy which, moreover, bore the ring with Elphin's own seal. When

Elphin was summoned from his tower cell to see the ring he immediately owned that it was the one he had given to his wife.

Seeing Elphin's evident distress, the king grew lenient. Believing that he had taught Elphin a hard lesson, he forgave the young man's rashness and started to offer prudent advice against trusting anyone when they are out of sight . . .

Elphin, though, interrupted the king.

"The ring belongs to my lady, yes. But the finger does not!"

"Then you maintain your boast?"

Unbeknownst to Elphin, the king or the prince, it was Taliesin who had anticipated the attempted seduction. He had advised Elphin's wife to dress a serving girl in her likeness, and to give her jewels and rings in plenty. And so it was the wench, thus attired, that was sent to entertain the prince while the lady of the house had discreetly stayed out of sight and out of trouble. Taliesin knew that the prince often resorted to drugging his victims in order to get his way.

Elphin was obviously confused but he was not dismayed.

"I cannot explain the finger in the ring," he said. "But my wife's virtue is not at fault."

The king, though, was filled with fury at Elphin's apparent impudence. Vowing that he would rot there until Elphin himself proved the accuracy of his boasts, the king had him thrown back into the tower!

Taliesin Goes to Court

~

Aware that his master languished once more in jail, Taliesin sought and obtained his lady's permission to undertake the journey to the king's court.

Once there, he quietly settled down close to the door where the bards would enter the great hall for the evening feast.

At the appropriate time the king's twenty-four bards, led by Heinin Vardd the chief bard, entered solemnly. None of them took much notice of the lad as he crouched in the corner by the door. And each and every one of them ignored the youth's apparent insolence as he pouted at them, playing "Blerum, blerum" on his lips with his finger as they passed by.

When they stood before the court to address the king, however, one and all could do nothing else than pout and play "Blerum,

blerum" on their lips with their fingers!

The king was troubled, supposing them to be intoxicated, and sent a messenger to remind them of where they were and what was appropriate for their position.

The bards persisted in their strange behavior, however, and the king sent another messenger to impress upon them the unseemliness of their actions.

Still the bards continued their bizarre antics, and the king sent a third messenger to ask them to reconsider their conduct.

With nothing changed, the king despatched a squire to convince them of the error of their ways. The squire headed straight for Heinin and, sensing insult in his attitude, thwacked him smartly over the head with a broom!

The Word Storm

~

Heinin, the chief bard, raised himself up from where he had been knocked down, and, falling immediately to his knees, beseeched the king for forgiveness.

With a crooked finger the old bard pointed to the shadows where Taliesin waited.

The squire was ordered to fetch the lad, who was then commanded to account for himself.

With a long and riddling speech the youth proclaimed himself the chief bard of Elphin and the best bard in the land.

When the king heard this he commanded Heinin to answer the challenge. But all Heinin could muster was another chorus of "Blerum, blerum!" And the refrain was earnestly taken up by every one of the other courtly bards.

Then Taliesin whipped up a storm of

words to buffet the ears of the sycophantic bards and thunder in the minds of the flattery-loving court. His compelling enchantment was echoed outside the hall by a growing wind that billowed freezing drafts through every crevice.

Before he had finished, he had brewed a gale as great as any could remember. The courtiers were terrified that a legion of demons were howling around the fortress, preparing to tear off the roof!

The Second Caldron

~

With even his bards cowering, the king despaired and called for his men to fetch Elphin.

All the power of the wind was channeled by Taliesin's incantation to shatter instantly the chains that had shackled his lord.

In the sudden silence that followed, Taliesin brought Elphin's wife out from where she too had waited in the shadows. When the king saw her delicate hands with their fingers all intact, he wondered how the coarse digit that his son had taken had ever been mistaken for a lady's.

While the king was engaged in this shameful recollection, Taliesin spurred Elphin to declare that he owned a horse that was faster than any in the land.

Bewildered but resolute, the king accepted this direct challenge, and without a moment's delay he commanded that his aides arrange a horse race.

The king was taking no chances and fielded fully twenty-four of his best steeds to Elphin's one contender.

Just before the race began, Taliesin took Elphin's jockey aside. The rider was instructed to hold back until he had been passed by all the king's horses, and then to make up ground.

Elphin was perplexed indeed at the start of the race, when he saw his horse fall behind and bring up the rear. Then he was mystified as he watched his jockey making up ground and, as he passed a horse, he struck it once with a twig.

These twigs had been given to the jockey by Taliesin: one for each of the king's horses. They were each of holly wood (which Taliesin had burnt until it was black), and the jockey dropped each as soon as he had used it.

Furthermore, Elphin was appalled when he saw his mount stumble and nearly fall, and amazed when he saw his jockey deliberately toss his cap to the ground at that very spot!

The jockey vied valiantly for position among the herd, and had indeed successfully dropped all twenty-four sticks before he reached the finish.

Elphin had scarcely fully realized his victory, however, before Taliesin gave the command for spades to be brought, and he marched across the course to where the jockey's fallen cap lay on the bruised grass.

Although the digging was difficult in the frost-hardened soil, the workmen delved deeply at their lord's behest.

As the men uncovered a caldron, Taliesin spoke to Elphin saying, "Here is payment for lifting me from the salmon weir and raising me in your household."

As Elphin stooped down to lift the lid he

saw the mighty vessel was crammed with gold.

From that time forward Taliesin's fame spread far and wide: he advised kings on many subtle matters, starting at the court wherein he stood; and his prowess as a poet divinely inspired was without equal anywhere in the land.

PWYLL, A FLAWED LORD

~

Pwyll, Lord of Dyfed (southwest Wales) was not always famed for his intelligence – his wits would sometimes desert him at crucial moments – but his loyalty and sense of honor were keen.

One morning he was at Arberth, the site of his chief court, when his mind turned to hunting. That very evening he rode with his companions toward Glynn Cuch, rested the night and, in the early morning light, blew on his horn and loosed his hounds into the forest.

In the chase he became separated from his companions and, in a clearing in the greenwood, suddenly heeded the hue and cry of another pack hunting in this, his own, hunting ground. All at once a stag stumbled into the glade and was overcome by the hounds, but no ordinary dogs were these – their ears were red as the freshest blood, and their coats were white as snow!

Nevertheless, he drove them away and set his own hounds to feast on the antlered corpse. Then the master of the strange pack rode up on a gray horse: he too was dressed in gray.

"You have shown me great discourtesy," said the gray man in a voice that suited his clothes. "It is dishonorable to bait your hounds upon the stag brought down by these hounds of mine."

Guessing that this was no ordinary man, Pwyll was cautious. "Tell me your name, that we may become friends."

"I am Arawn, king of Annwvyn. But friends we may never be until you atone for the insult you have done me."

"How may I earn your friendship?"

"I will cloak you in glamor so that all my countrymen looking upon you see only me, and I will send you to Annwvyn to rule in my stead for a year and a day. You may sleep with the most beautiful woman in my realm and enjoy all the finest fruits of my kingdom for a year — but on the final day you must meet a deadly rival in single combat."

"Very well," said Pwyll. "But what of mine own kingdom?"

"I shall rule it likewise, in your place and in your likeness."

"So be it."

Pwyll Faces the Unknown Foe

~

Arawn guided Pwyll into Annwvyn until they could see a magnificent court, whereupon Arawn bade Pwyll farewell and headed for Arberth.

Pwyll was enchanted both with the riches of the palace and with the nobility of the courtiers, and his queen was indeed the most beautiful woman he had ever seen. They passed the evening together in the company of a mighty host carousing in a great hall, accompanied by the songs from bards of unsurpassable skill.

When the time came for retiring to bed, however, Pwyll was doubly cautious. In bed he turned away from the queen, and gave the appearance of sleeping as soon as his head was laid down. In the morning he resumed his active enjoyment of all the delights of the court (which included much

hunting), but at night again he grew quiet.
And so it was every day and night for a year.

On the last day he rose and assembled his
nobles. They rode together to the edge of the
realm, where the neighboring king had
arranged to meet them to decide the future
ownership of the kingdoms.

In mortal combat they met in the middle
of the ford of a river that was the boundary
between their lands. They rushed at each
other, and Pwyll's first sword stroke cleft his
opponent's shield and bit mortally deep into
the flesh behind.

"I do not know you!" cried the wounded
king. "Neither do I know why you have
fought me, but finish now what you have
begun – slay me outright."

Although his disguise was not effective
against this erstwhile invader, Pwyll saw that
his one powerful blow had achieved all that
Arawn had asked. "I will show you mercy, but
demand the allegiance of all your followers,

that these two realms should be united and ruled from my court."

Powerless to prevent it, the foreign king gave up his crown, and Pwyll departed in peace, having doubled the size of the kingdom he had ruled for a year and a day.

When Pwyll met Arawn they exchanged likenesses and repaired to their own lands again. When Arawn entered his queen's bed and caressed her lovingly she chided him for his untoward passion, and he realized Pwyll had resisted her charms. He told her the whole story and they marveled together at Pwyll's honor.

When Pwyll returned to Arberth he learned that never had the realm been more wisely governed, and that prosperity was abundant throughout the land. He too confided in his friends, who openly asked him not to countermand the changes Arawn had made, and Pwyll assured them he would try to be as wise as his friend.

Each year Pwyll and Arawn exchanged gifts of hawks, hounds, horses, and whatever other treasures they hoped the other might enjoy. And Pwyll, Lord of Dyfed, was ever after known as Pwyll, Head of Annwvyn.

Pwyll Sees a Wonder

～

There is a strange legend about the Mound of Arberth, which rises above Pwyll's court. Whenever a man of royal blood sits upon it he will either be severely beaten or will see a wondrous thing . . .

Early one evening, Pwyll was feasting with his court when he grew listless and was tempted to test the legend. He set off with a few select companions and settled down to hold his vigil atop the Mound.

Not long passed though before a woman, richly dressed in shining gold brocade, rode toward them along the highway that ran past the Mount. Although Pwyll lost no time in sending a messenger to ask the identity of this comely stranger riding through their midst, by the time the herald had run down to the highway she was already past. And, try as he might, he could not catch up with her, even though she was not hurrying.

His interest piqued, Pwyll despatched a rider to fetch a horse and follow the woman.

All the while, the woman on her great pale horse rode – almost gliding – casually along. But show his horse the spur as mightily as he dared, still the messenger could not draw near!

Indeed, Pwyll had seen a wondrous sight, but he left the Mound more perplexed than content.

The next day, at the very same time, he chose the same companions to accompany him back to the Mound – there to sit and await who knows what? But Pwyll had ordered the fastest horse in the royal stables to be brought with them.

And his hope was not disappointed, for the same woman in shining raiment appeared along the highway. Strangely, though, by the time the messenger had mounted his horse and settled into the saddle, the woman was already opposite them.

Her pace was so leisurely that he felt sure to catch her even at a walk, and he was greatly surprised to find that he grew no closer. But greater still was his amazement when, even breaking into a gallop and giving his horse its head, she seemed to drift ever further away.

He returned, defeated, but Pwyll was wise enough not to scorn his efforts. Being of royal blood he knew the wonder was not intended merely to vex his messengers, but was surely meant for him. Again they returned thoughtfully to the feast at court.

Pwyll Meets the Wondrous Woman

~

At the same time the next day, as before Pwyll and his companions went to the Mound, and this time he ordered his own horse to be made ready and accompany them.

As soon as he sat on the hill, the woman appeared exactly as before. But by the time he had leaped into his saddle she had already drawn level, and as he spurred his prancing horse down the hill her back was already turned to him.

Although she seemed but a few paces away, and riding as slowly as the Moon, Pwyll could not catch her. "Lady!" He cried in exasperation. "For the sake of the man you love most, halt for me!"

"Gladly I will!" Her voice was like song as she spoke teasingly. "It would have gone easier on your horse had you asked me sooner."

She lifted the veil from over her face, and Pwyll saw the beauty of every maiden he had ever seen, shining in her eyes. "My name is Rhiannon, and my father is giving me to a man I have not chosen. I love you, and I will go to no other unless you reject me now."

"If every maiden in all the world were assembled here for me now, I would choose swiftly and certainly, and I would choose you!"

"Then come to my father's court one year from tonight, and we shall feast and be glad of each other!"

Pwyll Gives Away his Own Bride!

~

While minutes passed slowly, the year sped by, and soon enough Pwyll sat between Rhiannon and her father overlooking a mighty assembly seated each according to rank, and feasting with obvious pleasure.

As customary, bards and entertainers were showered with gifts for their talents, and suppliants also were admitted to be heard. As guest of honor, Pwyll had the pleasure of satisfying the worthy requests. One such young man, auburn-haired and handsome, entered nobly and modestly asked for a favor.

"Whatever you ask," said Pwyll. "If it is in my power, you shall have it."

"No!" shrieked Rhiannon.

"Yes, lady," answered the youth coyly. "Lord Pwyll has given his word."

"Friend?" queried Pwyll, sensing some

drastic mistake. "What do you want?"

"Rhiannon is the woman I love most. I want her to be mine, and to sit where you sit now, at the head of this feast!"

"It is well you have fallen silent," Rhiannon chided Pwyll. "Though I doubt even your feeble wits could do more damage. This is Gwawl, the man my father had chosen for me – and you have given me to him!

"Gwawl, the feast is not Pwyll's to give, but I shall give you another. And as for me, because he has given up his claim, I will be yours – come here in one year from tonight, and I will await your pleasure."

Gwawl was satisfied and departed in triumph. But Pwyll and his courtiers did not leave in despair, for Rhiannon had hatched a plan . . .

Pwyll Reclaims his Bride

~

One year later, as Gwawl enjoyed the hearty feast laid in his honor, Pwyll lurked outside the hall, garbed in the rag boots and tattered garb of an itinerant beggar. In an orchard nearby, however, ninety-nine of his finest warriors awaited his signal.

When the carousing had begun in earnest and generosity flowed with the wine, Pwyll slipped inside and approached Gwawl, guest of honor. "Lord," he begged when Gwawl noticed the shabby figure. "I am a suppliant."

"I will grant any wish you make, within reason," said Gwawl, naturally cautious.

"I wish only that you fill my bag with provisions for my journey."

The request was no sooner agreed than servants started piling in food of all descriptions. But however much they poured in, the bag grew no fuller.

When Gwawl noticed, he marveled: "Can your bag never be full up?"

"Lord, it is a wondrous thing, but not until a rich and powerful nobleman presses the food down with both feet, can this bag be filled."

"My nobleman!" cried Rhiannon in jest. "Go at once and prove your worth!"

In a bound Gwawl was standing with both feet in the bag. In a trice Pwyll tipped it up and pulled the drawstring shut. His horn brayed out its signal and in an instant the hall was filled with his warriors bristling with glinting weapons.

"Let me out!" cried Gwawl, for it seemed to him that each of Pwyll's warriors had beaten him severely as they entered the hall.

Rhiannon advised Pwyll to make Gwawl agree to accept defeat, seek no vengeance, and – for the duration of the feast at which Pwyll was now guest of honor – to settle all requests from whosoever might beg any favors!

Pwyll took her advice. Gwawl accepted the terms and left in search of a healing bath.

Rhiannon and Pwyll left her father's house to take up residence at the court of Arberth. There was great feasting indeed when the couple arrived, and all who came to see Rhiannon received wondrous gifts of precious jewelry, whether they asked for anything or not.

Rhiannon Accused of Murder

~

When Pwyll and Rhiannon had been together for three years yet had produced no offspring, people began to talk, and his advisers grew anxious lest he should have no heir. But before another year was past, at their court at Arberth, she bore him a son. Mother and child were well, and great was the rejoicing at the feast that night.

Rhiannon had six women to attend her and the baby in her chamber during that night, but the lures of fatigue weighed strangely heavily on them, and all six fell fast asleep before midnight.

When they awoke at dawn Rhiannon was still sleeping, but the child was nowhere to be found!

They realized at once that all the blame for the child's disappearance would fall on them, and that they would count themselves lucky to escape with a mercifully quick execution. One among them suggested an alternative.

"We could say that Rhiannon destroyed the child herself: it will be her word against ours — and there are six of us. There is a deerhound with a litter of pups: we could slay some of them, smear blood on her hands and face, and scatter bones about her bed — the evidence would support our claims."

When Rhiannon awoke to a scene of carnage she was distraught, but she did not believe their lies.

"Wretches, why have you invented this story? Surely if you knew what had become of my son you would tell me straight, so if somehow you do not know what has happened then be honest and confess it — you need fear no punishment for I will protect you if you tell the truth."

The six faithless women did not dare to admit their conspiracy, and Rhiannon was condemned before Pwyll, the court, and all the people of Dyfed . . .

The Disappearing Foals

~

Meanwhile, another mystery was about to yield a strange harvest.

Teirnon Twrvliant, lord of Gwent Below the Woods, was the proud owner of a mare that was the most handsome in the land. Yet despite years of trying, he had never succeeding in raising even one of her foals.

She produced a foal on the same date every year: Beltane, the eve of May Day — when the boundary between the realms of men and the otherworld are mighty thin and easily crossed. Each year by morning the foal had simply disappeared.

This year, though, he determined to discover what was happening, so he armed himself and commenced a vigil. Sure enough, his mare foaled as night fell, and the colt got straight to its feet, and was peerless in perfection.

As he inspected the sturdy animal he heard a sudden commotion outside, and a massive clawed hand crashed through the window, seizing the colt by the mane!

In an instant Teirnon's sword was drawn and he hacked off the arm at the elbow, saving the colt from being taken.

Although deafened by the creature's shrieks of pain, Teirnon rushed outside to press the fight, but the beast had vanished into the night. Turning to go back indoors he noticed a bundle beside the door.

Hastily making the mare and her foal comfortable, Teirnon rushed to his wife with the bundle in his arms.

"Lady, are you asleep?"

"I was, deeply, but you have wakened me."

"I have here the one thing you have always wished for!"

Gently he gave the bundle to her. It was a silk mantle – wrapped around a baby boy cocooned in swaddling clothes.

Her eyes were gleaming with joy and moist with love.

"I could say that I have been secretly pregnant," she suggested.

"So be it."

Rhiannon's Punishment

~

Although she never believed that she could have been guilty of devouring her baby, Rhiannon accepted her punishment with fortitude.

Every day for four years she sat at the main entrance to Arberth, telling her story to all who had not heard it before. She also had to offer to carry on her back any willing stranger or guest from the gate to the court itself. And there were those who, hearing her tale, zealously accepted the ride.

When travelers returning from Arberth told Teirnon what fate had stricken Rhiannon, he was deeply moved. The child they had claimed as their own had grown marvelously fast – by the time he was a year old he was running rings around three-year-olds; a year later he was besting six-year-olds; by the time he was four he was vying with the stablehands to care for the horses. Indeed, the colt that had been born and rescued the night he had arrived, was given to him for his very own.

As Teirnon gazed at his adopted son he remembered Pwyll (for he had once worked in his court), and realized that the boy unquestionably bore the likeness of Pwyll, Head of Annwvyn.

Though it grieved her, his wife willingly gave up her ward and returned him to the life he had never known.

"Halt," cried Rhiannon as they rode through the gate of Arberth.

"I will carry each of you on my back into court, as this is my punishment for seven years, for brutally slaying my baby son."

"Lady," said Teirnon, smiling. "That will not be necessary..."

Great was the feasting that night when the boy was revealed to Pwyll and Rhiannon in front of the entire court, for there was no doubt in anyone's mind that this was the missing child. As was the custom, the mother gave her son his name – having been a source of desperate worry and heartache for so long, she called him Pryderi, that is, Anxiety.

And great was the rejoicing throughout Dyfed, both because Pwyll had an heir once again, and also that Rhiannon's bitter disgrace was ended. The lighthearted joy of relief was felt in every breast . . . every breast except six that is. For them, the false-hearted women, the name Pryderi meant doom!

BRAN AND BRANWEN

~

Bran the Blessed, the son of Llyr, was king of the Island of the Mighty, as Britain was known. He was a giant of a man, and immensely strong, but also prudent and took care to abuse neither his strength nor his position.

Bran had a sister, Branwen, the most beautiful maiden in the world. Her fame spread far and wide, and one day Mallolwch, king of Ireland, came seeking her hand . . .

Bran and his nobles were in the open air at his court in Harlech when thirteen ships were spied running swiftly before the west wind, coming from the south of Ireland. At once Bran gathered the warriors of the court and sent them to meet the vessels.

The leading ship was even more exquisitely

wrought than its fellows, graceful, and with ensigns of rich brocade. On its deck was a shield, with its point uppermost as a token of peace.

From his vantage point above the strand, Bran greeted the strangers courteously. Malloluch expressed his wish to visit with Bran and Branwen, and proposed an alliance between the royal house of Ireland and the Island of the Mighty.

Bran's council advised acceptance, and a great feast was prepared in celebration of the union of Malloluch and Branwen, Ireland and Britain. The festivities took place in tents — no hall had ever been built that was large enough to house Bran!

However, they had neglected to tell Evnissyen (half-brother to both Bran and Branwen) that his sister was being given away. When he found out, the morning after the feast, his too-quick temper blazed with wrath at being slighted, and he lashed out at the nearest living things — the king of Ireland's horses!

When his rage was spent, there was not a beast remaining that was not horribly maimed.

When Mallolwch discovered the dreadful abuse of his precious animals, he felt grievously insulted and, taking Branwen with him, marched his men to their ships, vowing vengeance.

Hearing what had happened, Bran sent his herald to make peace with Mallolwch, offering him compensation. Not only was there to be a replacement horse for each one mutilated but, as tokens of good will, a staff of silver as thick as Mallolwch's little finger and as tall as the Irish king himself, and a disc of gold as broad as his face.

Mallolwch accepted the offer and returned to his place of honor at the feast. But Bran still felt embarrassed because he could not punish Evnissyen (who was his own mother's son), so he gave Mallolwch a magic caldron . . .

The Caldron of Rebirth

~

This caldron had been carried out of the depths of a lake in Ireland, on the back of a strange, giant man. The giant's even larger wife — an unnatural woman who gave birth to fully armed warriors — followed him from the lake.

The outlandish family soon earned a reputation for outrageous behavior and were hated far and wide, but because of their strength and fighting spirit they could not be openly challenged.

At length the local people contrived to get them drunk and lure them inside a newly built house, offered as a gift to shelter their growing family. But the walls and roof were made of iron and, as soon as the family were asleep, the men barred the exits, heaped charcoal all around it, and proceeded to bake them all.

When the walls became white-hot however, the iron grew weak, and the man barged his way through. Although the children perished, he escaped with his wife and the caldron to Britain. Welcomed and now well behaved, his family prospered and, in gratitude, he gave the magic vessel to Bran.

When Mallolwch heard that if a slain warrior were tossed into the caldron he would rise again the next morning and be fit to fight again (except he would have no voice), he took part in the feast as gladly as on the night before.

Branwen in Ireland

~

There was great feasting when Branwen arrived at her new home in Ireland. She showered gifts on all who came to greet her, and everyone rejoiced.

In due course she bore Mallolwch a son, Gwern, who was sent to be fostered at the best place in the land. But her own standing began to slip, and the courtiers began to complain about her, remembering her half-brother's savage attack on their horses.

At length she was exiled from the king's chamber and sent to work in the kitchens where she was cruelly taunted. For three years she suffered blows at the butcher's hands, and her only companion was a starling she had raised from a chick, and kept safely hidden in her kneading trough.

She told it all her woes and, when it

could speak, she sent it to fly over the sea to Bran . . .

It was not long after that swineherds, who had been fattening their pigs by the strand, ran into the Irish king's court bearing tales of a great wonder.

"We have seen a forest growing out of the sea, with a mountain in its midst, and atop that mountain was a great ridge with a lake on either side – and they are all moving toward our land!"

Branwen knew the answer to this riddle. The forest was the masts of a mighty avenging fleet, and the mountain was Bran himself, wading across the Irish Sea – the ridge and lakes were his nose and eyes!

In fear, the king and his men fell back from the coast but left heralds to parley with Bran. They told him that, to avoid terrible slaughter on both sides, Mallolwch would immediately renounce the throne of Ireland in favour of Gwern, who would be invested as king in the presence of Bran and his entire company. Furthermore, the heralds said, a special building for the festivities would be raised – the first hall ever to be large and sturdy enough to house Bran.

Branwen herself, not wanting the land laid to waste and her adopted folk slaughtered, agreed the terms of the treaty, and Bran accepted them also.

From Peace to War

~

The building was raised upon one hundred pillars, but the Irish dealt falsely with their guests, and hung a leather sack from each pillar. Within each sack was a warrior, ready to leap forth upon the British when they were wearied from the night's carousing, but Evnissyen sensed an ambush and asked a steward what the sacks contained. Hearing that they contained flour, he slipped his hand into each to test its fineness -- and crushed the skulls of every one of the hundred hiding men.

Enraged at the treacherous attack the Irish had planned, Evnissyen grabbed Gwern, and thrust him headlong to his death in the great fireplace!

In an instant the feast was transformed into a battlefield. Although the warriors from the Island of the Mighty fought fiercely, the Irish kindled a fire to heat the magic caldron, and every corpse they put into it came out ready to fight afresh the next morning.

Evnissyen saw that the fight was unequal, and lamented that yet again his rage had sparked a conflict. He put aside his native apparel and disguised himself as an Irish warrior, and lay himself down as if slain on the field of combat. When he too was plunged into the caldron of rebirth, he stretched his limbs and broke it asunder. His brave heart burst also as the caldron fell in four twisted parts.

The Assembly of the Wondrous Head

~

The remaining fighters from the Island of the Mighty defeated the Irish host, but only seven of them left the battle alive. Bran himself had been dealt a mortal blow by a poisoned spear that pierced his foot. Dying, he gave his friends instructions for his funeral and, bizarre though they sounded, they were carried out without question.

They cut his head from his body and, taking Branwen with them, returned to Wales. On her native soil, Branwen broke down and mourned for the two nations who had lost their finest men – all for her sake – and she perished, brokenhearted, from pure grief.

The company of seven and the head -- which had lost neither its wits nor power of speech – moved toward Harlech and heard along the way that there was now a new king over Britain. Bran's son (who had ruled in his absence) had died of grief at the sight of his friends being hacked apart by a sword – a sword alone – for the usurper was wrapped in a magic cloak of invisibility!

At Harlech the company of seven marveled as the three birds of Rhiannon appeared and began to sing. From far across the ocean they sang, yet they seemed close at hand, and so sweet were their melodies that the company spent seven happy years rapt in wonder.

Then they set out for a royal hall at Gwales which had three doors, one of which was shut. Here, for eighty years, they made merry and enjoyed the companionship of the wondrous head, and none of them grew older by so much as a single day!

At length, though, as Bran had foretold, one among them suddenly grew curious to open the third door. It opened onto a vista of the Bristol Channel and Cornwall, and straight away the Assembly of the Wondrous Head – as they were ever after known – were stricken with all the pain of grief for their dead kinsmen.

Now in deepest mourning, they carried the head of Bran the Blessed to London and buried it in the White Hill where, for as long as it remained secret, it served to protect the Island of the Mighty from all manner of plagues from across the seas.

MANAWYDAN AND THE ENCHANTMENT OF DYFED

~

Having buried both his sister, Branwen, and his brother Bran, Manawydan was at a crossroads in his life, but didn't know which way to turn. As it turned out, he was about to embark on a strange and wondrous adventure.

He shared his grief with his friend Pryderi, whose father, Pwyll, had died, and whose mother, the widow Rhiannon, had since met no one with whom she wished to share her life.

Sensing that Rhiannon might enjoy the company of the noble veteran, and vice versa, Pryderi invited Manawydan to join him at their court. Having no business to take him elsewhere, and persuaded by the prospect of pleasant companionship, Manawydan accepted.

Fine was the feast that Rhiannon and Kigva, Pryderi's wife, prepared for them. And as the four talked, Manawydan found himself looking at Rhiannon more and more tenderly, until he realized that she was the most lovely woman he had ever seen. And she too was glad in her heart when Pryderi openly declared that he had indeed played the matchmaker.

That night they retired together to her chamber, and the morning found them joyously inseparable.

The following weeks they wandered widely through the rich countryside of Dyfed. The hunting was the best Manawydan had known, the rivers teemed with fish and the honey was as sweet as their happy journey together through this land of delights . . .

The Great Desolation

~

When they had completed their round of Dyfed, the four returned to Arberth, the chief court of the realm. From here Pryderi issued the declaration for celebrations throughout the land, in honor of Manawydan and Rhiannon.

The first evening there, they made a fateful decision. Part way through the festivities the four arose and, in a quiet conspiracy, they slipped out of the banqueting hall.

Their goal, soon reached, was to scale the summit of the Mound of Arberth. Anyone of royal blood who sat atop this sacred site, as Pryderi's father had verified, would either be severely beaten, or would see a great wonder. They did not have to wait long before their destiny befell them.

Thunder rumbled around them, as if

announcing the approach of a quickly thickening mist that soon engulfed them utterly as the thunder grew louder. The darkness was such that none could see the other, and any cry was lost in the deafening roar.

Almost as quickly as it fell though, the mist lifted, and their ears were left ringing in the swiftly fallen silence.

It was night no longer, but day. Yet the vista that lay below them was scarcely recognizable. In place of the fields, the flocks, herds, and farmsteads with thin blue ribbons of smoke spiraling idly from their roofs - the land was bare and laid waste of both man and beast. Even the great hall of the court was desolate, ruined and utterly deserted.

The four were alone.

The Struggle to Make a Living
~

Pryderi and Manawydan were successful in
the hunt, while Kigva and Rhiannon
together contrived to make their plight seem
a delight. The couples spent not one, but two
years like this, such was their happiness
together.

At length though, they set off to follow
the road out of Dyfed, to see what they might
find.

At Hereford they settled awhile and,
enjoying the company and comforts,
Manawydan suggested they take up
saddlemaking. They modelled their wares on
the best they had ever seen, and such was the
quality of their saddles that soon nobody in
the town bought from anyone else unless
Manawydan had run out of stock.

When the established saddlers of
Hereford realized this they determined to

kill the newcomers. A kindly word, however, alerted the four to the threat and, although Pryderi thought to stand and fight, they chose to move to another town.

Once settled, they took up the craft of shieldmaking, again using the best their memories could conjure as models for their designs. Soon no one bought shields from any other supplier, so long as Manawydan had stocks to sell.

Once the local shieldmakers saw their trade disappear they grew angry and afraid, and determined to kill the newcomers.

When Pryderi heard about this threat, he wanted to face them in combat, but Manawydan counseled them to move on to another town, and so they did.

Although there they made shoes, thinking the other shoemakers would be a less martial company, they were mistaken, and again they had little choice but to leave.

The Enchanted Fortress

~

The four friends decided to abandon
the troublesome towns, and returned
to the deserted but peaceful court of
Arberth.

Settling quickly back into the routine of
hunting and gathering to support
themselves, the weeks soon became months,
and the months quickly turned full circle
and became a year.

One day, the men were out hunting with a
pack of dogs they had bought from the town,
when the animals started baying wildly at a
small copse of trees. The fiercest hounds
entered but retreated at once, cowering in
abject fear and with their tails firmly
between their legs.

As Manawydan and Pryderi rode toward
it, in an instant a shining white boar broke
from cover and bolted. It soon stopped

running however, and turned to face them, completely ignoring the hounds that snarled between them.

When the men rode closer to better view this strange creature, it wheeled and darted away once more. Again it stopped in open ground, defying the bloodthirsty hounds, and tantalizing the hunters.

This strange chase led the friends to mount the crest of a ridge and there, atop the highest point of the hill, rose a towering stone fortress where there had been no building before. The boar ran in at the open gate, closely followed by the hunting dogs.

Manawydan and Pryderi thought better of rushing in, and stood their ground to see what might befall their pack. As silence reigned though, Pryderi grew increasingly impatient, and would not willingly give up his dogs without an attempt to retrieve them.

"If you heed my advice," suggested Manawydan, "you will not enter here, for surely it is the work of the one who laid this enchantment of desolation over all the land."

If he was spurred to seek vengeance for the harrowing of his realm, Pryderi did not admit it, and simply replied, "I will not forsake my dogs."

He rode boldly forward toward the great gate set in the thick wall of the mighty fortress. As he thought to enter the courtyard however, he saw neither buildings, people, dogs nor the mysterious boar. Instead he found himself staring at a resplendent fountain paved around with marble, in what should have been the middle of the fortress.

Above one of the slabs of marble hung a bowl of gold, suspended from four fine chains which reached into the air so far that no mortal eye could see their source.

Stricken with the beauty of the golden bowl, Pryderi strode across the paving and reached out to touch it, marveling at its exquisite workmanship.

As soon as he touched it though, his hands stuck fast, his feet became rooted to the slab on which he stood, and his tongue froze so he could not utter a sound.

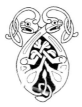

Then There Were Two...

~

After waiting until nightfall for any sign of his friend, Manawydan arrived back at the makeshift court of Arberth in a state of dejection.

Despite the women's worry over the late return of the hunting party, his reception was not kind. Once Rhiannon heard about the fortress from which none returned, she bitterly cried, "You have been a bad friend – and have lost a good one!"

Without another word she rode off into the night to find her son. Soon enough she found the towering fortress, saw the gate standing wide open, and entered its gloomy walls. Once inside she too saw the fountain and there also stood Pryderi, clasping the shining golden bowl.

"My lord, what are you doing?" she begged as she approached, and before she could see what was amiss she too had put out her hand and touched the bowl beside his fingertips.

In a trice she too was caught fast.

Thunder rumbled around them as mist rolled over the hill, completely enveloping the enchanted fortress, and then it vanished, never to be seen again. Rhiannon and Pryderi had disappeared.

A Bitter Harvest

~

Kigva was distraught at the loss of her husband, crying, "To live like this is worse than it would be to be dead!"

But Manawydan was a better friend to Pryderi than Rhiannon had given him credit for, and he respected his friend's wife as though he were still with them. To Manawydan, Pryderi was not dead and gone, but merely traveling in some distant land, eagerly expected home any day.

He was no fool though, and, keenly feeling the loss of the hunting dogs, set about providing for the two of them by turning the soil and sowing wheat in three crofts.

As the seasons turned from spring to autumn, the wheat grew tall and straight in the fertile earth, and ripened well in the favorable climate.

With the weather set fair and the first croft ready for reaping, Manawydan retired early, so as to be ready for a hard day's work in the field. He slept soundly and went to the croft as soon as the dew was dry, but when he arrived he found a field of standing stalks – with not an ear of wheat to be seen anywhere upon them!

Dismayed but not disheartened, he turned away to inspect the second croft. This, he found, was undamaged and would be ripe for harvesting the next day.

The next day though, he again found bare stalks and a harvest stolen completely away. Lamenting his losses and wasted work, he moved on to check the third remaining croft. This was intact and ready for the harvest tomorrow.

Thieves in the Night

~

Manawydan gathered his weapons and set himself to watch the last remaining croft all night, for without a store of grain they would suffer cruel need during the long winter months, and he determined to defend it as long as he was able.

At midnight he was swept up in an abyss of commotion and din, and when he regained his balance he saw the field was alive with the greatest host of mice ever seen.

Try as he might he could no more seek and destroy a single mouse than a hawk could hunt quarry from a swarm of gnats. Before his eyes, blazing with wrath, he saw the furry creatures scurry up each stalk in the croft, and nip off every ear.

As the scampering tide turned to run away, each mouse with an ear clenched in its teeth, Manawydan caught sight of one which was larger than the others and moved more slowly. His anger lent him the instincts of a cat and in a trice he pounced and caught it up. A moment later he dropped it into his empty glove and tied the wristband with a thong.

When he returned to their abode in the abandoned court, Kigva quizzed him about the glove he carried with the air of a trophy.

"This," he explained, "is a thief, one of many that came to steal our harvest — and took it all! I wish that I had caught more of them, but this one at least shall pay the price for the crime. I shall hang it in the morning."

When Kigva heard that the plunderer was a mere mouse, she complained that to handle such a base creature would bring dishonor to his rank and dignity. But Manawydan was adamant.

"If you had any good reason to plead on

behalf of this creature I would listen to your counsel, but as you have none to offer, I shall do as I say and destroy it in the morning.

For the Sake of a Mouse . . .

~

Dawn found Manawydan sitting atop the Mound of Arberth, setting up a pair of forked sticks on the very highest point.

As he did so he was distracted by a man dressed in old, tattered clothes, on the road below. This was the first person Manawydan had seen in the realm, other than his three companions, for fully seven years.

The man enquired what he was doing atop the Mound. When Manawydan explained, the traveler offered to pay him a pound that he'd been given for singing, to avert the dishonor that such an execution would entail.

Manawydan refused, saying, "I caught it stealing, the penalty for stealing is hanging, and I intend to see justice done." At that, the scholar went on his way.

As Manawydan was fixing the crossbeam to the gallows, he was hailed by a priest sat upon a horse, richly arrayed, on the road below. Again the tale was told. The priest offered to buy the culprit for three pounds rather than watch the man hang the mouse.

"No, I will not accept any payment that is less than a thief deserves, which is to be hanged."

The priest went on his way, and Manawydan took the mouse from the glove and tied the thong around its neck. As he did so a bishop, at the head of a substantial baggage train, called up to him from the road below.

"Rather than see such a noble man debase his good character by handling such a worthless creature, I will give you all these seven loads of rich baggage and the horses that bear them, if you will free the mouse."

"I will not take that," replied Manawydan.

"Then name your price!" cried the traveler.

"I want Pryderi and Rhiannon to be free, and the enchantment of desolation that lies upon Dyfed to be removed!"

"You shall have all that. Now give the mouse to me."

"That is not all – who is this mouse?"

"She is my wife."

"What was she doing in my crofts?"

"Exacting vengeance for the savage beating of Gwawl at the wedding feast that should have celebrated his union with Rhiannon – but was usurped by Pwyll, Pryderi's father.

"Seeing your wheat ripe and ready for harvest, all of my people begged me to help them play a part in your downfall. I turned them all into mice to rob you so that you – Rhiannon's new consort, and Kigva, Pryderi's wife – would starve.

"My wife joined the host, but she is heavily pregnant, which is why you caught her when the others ran fast and free. Now, I

89

have answered your questions, let her go free."

"That is not all – promise both that Dyfed will remain free of evil enchantments, and also that you will allow no revenge to be taken on either Pryderi, Rhiannon or me."

"You shall have what you ask. Now let my wife come to me."

"Not until I see Pryderi and Rhiannon here."

"They are coming."

With that they appeared, and Manawydan rose to his feet to greet them.

Llwyd, for such was the enchanter's name, now asked again for his wife to be freed.

"Gladly!" cried Manawydan, and gently untied the knot and released the creature.

With a stroke of a magic wand Llwyd transformed the ungainly mouse back to its original form, and there stood the loveliest woman anyone had seen.

Then, to their great delight, all of the

court of Arberth reappeared in all its glory, both people, animals and buildings, and all as if they had never known a better day!

GWYDYON AND THE
OWL OF FLOWERS

~

Pitiful is the extremity of unrequited love, for treachery breeds in the tangle of hopes and fears that feather the nest of frustrated passion – especially when wizards meddle in affairs where angels would fear to tread . . .

Gwydyon, a wizard, was worried about his brother Gilvaethwy, and it didn't need second sight to see that something was wrong: the man had grown terribly pale recently, and was visibly wasting away.

"I fear I cannot say what is ailing me," said Gilvaethwy in reply to Gwydyon's enquiry. "For, as you know, our uncle Math has the gift of overhearing even the quietest whisper once it has been caught by the wind."

Math was lord of Gwynedd, north Wales, and Gwydyon and Gilvaethwy — his sister's sons — were second only to himself in power over the realm.

Gwydyon saw into his brother's heart and divined that Gilvaethwy was lovesick. The object of his desire, though, would not be easily won, for she was Goewin, Math's constant companion.

Moreover, Math would not willingly give her to any man. He had been cursed so that, except in time of war, he must have his feet resting in a virgin's lap — or else he would die. And Goewin was the maiden he had chosen to safeguard his life.

"Stop your sighing and pining," advised Gwydyon. "Nothing will be gained that way! I will devise a plan that will deliver her into your hands."

The Swine that Sparked a War

~

Gwydyon went to Math and told him that a new breed of animal "whose meat is better than that of oxen . . ." had arrived in Dyfed in the southwest of Wales. With honeyed words he keenly interested Math in these beasts – swine – that had been given to Pryderi, lord of Dyfed, by his late father's friend and long-standing ally Arawn, lord of the mysterious realm of Annwvyn.

No sooner had Math voiced his desire to own the creatures, if Gwydyon could obtain them, than the two nephews set off on the quest which they secretly hoped would deliver Goewin into Gilvaethwy's hands.

They traveled with ten close companions who were trusty warriors, and they were all dressed as bards. And when they arrived at Pryderi's court, Gwydyon was invited to entertain the assembly.

This was Gwydyon's plan, because a truly gifted bard could intoxicate his audience so that they would shower valuable gifts and treasures upon him. And Gwydyon's prowess in the telling of tales was unrivaled!

Before long, Pryderi was liberal with his gifts. But although Gwydyon approached the subject of the swine with great subtlety, barely mentioning that his request was made on Math's behalf, his proposition was politely though swiftly refused.

"I have solemnly undertaken neither to give away the swine nor sell them until they have bred twice their number," said Pryderi. "Otherwise I would gladly reward your wonderful stories."

"Perhaps tomorrow we will find a way to satisfy us both," replied Gwydyon.

False Bargain

~

That night Gwydyon wove spells with powerful incantations.

Taking twelve toadstools he conjured from each a splendid shield fit for a king. He used his magic arts to produce twelve glossy black greyhounds with snowy white breasts, and he provided them each with collars and leashes that gleamed like gold. Twelve magnificent stallions he also generated, with coloring identical to that of the hounds, and with saddles and bridles whose metalwork was all of gold.

Gwydyon sought out Pryderi early, and managed it so that the fabulous horses and hounds could be admired.

"Although you can neither give away the swine nor sell them outright," suggested Gwydyon, "perhaps these fine strong animals might interest you in making a fair exchange

— with these princely shields as a token of our pleasure in the trade?"

"This is a persuasive offer!" said Pryderi. "I am confident that my council will agree."

When the council did indeed ratify the terms of the transaction, Gwydyon mustered his men and drove the swine quickly away.

"We must make all speed, Gilvaethwy," he urged, "for by the middle of the night the horses and hounds will disappear, and the shields will turn back into toadstools."

"Pryderi will undoubtedly pursue us, bringing with him a host of doughty warriors intent on revenge — this will spark a war!"

"Exactly . . . "

The Passion, and the Combat
After the Slaughter

~

It took several days of travel to bring the swine safely into the heartland of Math's realm, and to settle them securely in a sty.

Then Gwydyon and Gilvaethwy returned to Math's court where they found the whole land was being mustered to arms, for Pryderi had roused his entire kingdom to retrieve the swine and exact dire vengeance for the disgraceful insult.

In haste, Math set off due south with his nobles and their armies, to meet the attacking army. That night Gwydyon and Gilvaethwy secretly returned to the court.

While Gwydyon removed and secured the few of Math's attendants who stood in their way, Gilvaethwy found himself alone with Goewin in Math's chamber. Against her will she was taken – and in the king's own bed, no less ...

At dawn the brothers rode hard to rejoin the company which was preparing for the onslaught of Pryderi's army.

The battle, once joined, was fierce and there was great slaughter on both sides. In time though, the invaders were forced to give ground. Their retreat was closely followed and the venture became a rout as they fled.

The southerners did regroup however, and sent messengers to sue for a truce. Accompanying them were twenty-four of the surviving nobility to serve as hostages.

Terms were agreed, and Pryderi and his men were escorted out of Math's kingdom. Along the way however, the whole grievous business rankled with the foot soldiers of the defeated side. They felt sorely the losses, both of brave men and good weapons, sustained in their efforts to right the shameful abuse of their lord's hospitality.

So many hotheaded skirmishes broke out that Pryderi feared they would escalate and force reprisals which would be nothing short of a massacre of his countrymen.

He sent word to Math that he wished to settle the matter once and for all time. He asked to meet Gwydyon man to man on the field of single combat, with the hosts standing back and accepting the outcome without further ado.

Gwydyon agreed to meet him, confident of his skill with spells to counter Pryderi's strong sword arm. They fought long and hard and it was indeed through his use of enchantments that Gwydyon won the day.

Pryderi was buried by his companions, who shed many a bitter tear before the vanquished host returned to their homes.

The Wizard is Spell-bound

With the war over, Math returned to his court and immediately sought out Goewin to lay his feet in her lap, lest his doom overtake him.

"Lord," she said, "You must find another virgin to tend your feet, for I cannot. I was assaulted: everyone here heard my cries, but Gilvaethwy raped me and dishonored you by using your very own bed."

Furious, Math vowed, "I will honor and protect you by taking you for my wife, which will give you authority over my realm. And I will seek compensation from my nephews both for the wrong they have done to you and the dishonor they have shown to me."

Gwydyon and Gilvaethwy had taken care to be far from the court when Math returned, but their safety was not assured. Math issued a proclamation that neither food nor drink be given to either of them, so that they must either chose self-imposed exile or be forced to return to court and submit to his judgment.

Assured both of his skill with words and his powers of enchantment, Gwydyon decided they should go to the court.

"We bow to your will," he said as they presented themselves to their uncle.

"You have cost our realm dear," thundered Math when they stood before him. "Despite our victory, we have lost many men and weapons. Your theft has shamed me, and the death of the noble Pryderi is entirely beyond my power to correct.

"Your escapades have allowed me time to consider your punishment, and now I will begin to punish you."

With those words he took up his magic wand and struck Gilvaethwy who was instantly transformed into a hind. Then he struck Gwydyon, who had tried to flee but found himself unable to move, and he became a stag.

"As your brotherly love has blinded you to greater loyalty, I shall make you closer still. You will run through the woods together as wild deer and, in the spring, you will return here."

The Nephew's Return

~

One night in the next year the court was roused by all the dogs barking into the darkness. Math was soon informed that three deer stood by the gates and, picking up his magic wand, he went to see them at once.

There he saw a stag, a hind, and a fawn.

Math lifted his wand to strike, saying, "The hind becomes a wild boar, the stag becomes a sow, the fawn becomes a boy who shall be properly fostered and cared for." And with three deft strokes of the wand the beasts were transfigured.

At the end of a year the dogs again bayed into the night, sensing wild animals by the gate. Math went to meet them and saw the boar, the sow, and a young boar.

With his wand at the ready he spoke.

The boar becomes a she-wolf, the sow

becomes a wolf, and the young boar becomes a boy who shall be properly fostered and cared for."

At a stroke the transformations took effect.

At the end of another year the court was again roused by the baying dogs scenting the presence of unnatural visitors. Again Math went to meet the creatures: wolf, she-wolf and wolf-cub.

"The wolf-cub becomes a boy who shall be properly fostered and cared for, the wolf and she-wolf shall be returned to their manly forms."

Gwydyon and Gilvaethwy stood there naked and disgraced, and Math saw that they had been punished enough.

Uncle Gwydyon

~

Having been responsible for depriving Math of Goewin's services, Gwydyon humbly suggested that a suitable replacement might be found in Aranrhod. Math looked on this contrite proposal kindly, and summoned Aranrhod, sister of Gwydyon and Gilvaethwy, to court.

When she arrived, Math determined to test if she were indeed a virgin. He took out his magic wand, bent it, and instructed Aranrhod to step over it.

As soon as she did so a baby boy with bright yellow hair fell from her with a cry. Aranrhod fled for the door and, as she did so, something else dropped also. Quickly, before anyone could see what the second thing was, Gwydyon picked it up and hid it discreetly. The baby boy was properly fostered and cared for.

What Gwydyon had picked up was indeed another child, and another boy. He had it fostered and nursed. By the end of a year the child was as large as a two-year-old, and by the end of the second year he was large enough to go to court, which is where Gwydyon took him. And, after a year at court, he was as large as a burly eight-year-old.

One day they went walking together and arrived at the Fortress of Aranrhod.

"Who is the boy, Gwydyon?" She asked.

"He is your son."

"You shame me by parading him here! What is his name?"

"He has no name as yet."

"Then I doom him to have none until I give it to him."

Aranrhod's Spite

~

Gwydyon was angered by Aranrhod's spiteful rejection of her son, and he took the child to the seashore opposite Anglesey, where they collected kelp and red seaweed. Conjuring a sailing ship to sail them to the harbor by the Fortress of Aranrhod, Gwydyon transformed the weeds into the finest soft leather, and then he changed their own appearance so that no one would recognize them.

As soon as they arrived they started trading as shoemakers, and word of their skill and beautiful leathers soon spread through the settlement, eventually reaching Aranrhod.

Intrigued, she let herself be persuaded to go and have her feet measured. As Gwydyon bent to cut the leather to fit her, and the boy was stitching, a wren alighted on the deck. In a trice the boy took aim and threw, piercing its leg between the sinew and the bone.

Aranrhod laughed. "It's a sure hand the light-haired one has!"

"Indeed," said Gwydyon straightening up. "And he has a fine name also: Lleu Sure Hand."

With that he raised the enchantment and all the leatherwork turned to seaweed, and Aranrhod saw who had tricked her.

"Well then, I doom him to have no weapons until I give them to him."

With that, Gwydyon and Lleu departed, not to return until Lleu was fully grown to manhood and well rehearsed with horsemanship and weaponry of all kinds, but still he had none to call his own.

Disguised as bards by Gwydyon's cunning magic, they sought admission at the gate of Fortress Aranrhod, and were received gladly. Aranrhod did not weary of Gwydyon's storytelling and it was late at night before they sought their separate chambers.

Early the next morning Gwydyon wrought his powers to produce a great commotion with trumpeting and panic throughout the land.

It was not long before he met Aranrhod, who told him that the sea was covered with ships bearing down on the Fortress. They soon agreed that there was nothing to do but secure the gates and defend themselves as best they might.

She gave orders that weapons be brought to arm the bards and, when they arrived, she herself promptly lent a hand in equipping the younger of the two men.

Amid the general clamor and confusion, Gwydyon softly enquired, "Is the lad's arming complete?"

"Indeed it is," she replied.

"Then we may put these weapons aside," said Gwydyon.

"But what of the invading fleet?"

"Their victory is already won, for you

Aranrhod, have armed your son!"

As the enchantment faded from her eyes, and she saw the truth of the matter, she grew angry and in fury swore, "I doom him to have no wife that is of any race on Earth!"

The Flower Maiden

~

Lacking magic strong enough to counter Aranrhod's dire curse, Gwydyon determined to seek the counsel of his uncle Math. When he heard the trials that Aranrhod had put in the path of her child, Math agreed to help.

Together, the two wizards gathered the flowers of oak, broom, and meadowsweet. With incantations and the power of their magic wands, they transformed these blossoms into the loveliest maiden they could imagine, and her beauty was utterly peerless.

They named her Blodeuedd and, at the wedding feast, Lleu was given a large and fertile stretch of land to support himself as lord. Once they had settled there the people grew to appreciate the wisdom with which he governed.

One day, while Lleu was paying a visit to

the court of Math, a huntsman rode past the court where Blodeuedd awaited her lord's return, in pursuit of a stag.

The huntsman was Goronwy, the lord of a neighboring region, and as dusk fell Blodeuedd was honor bound to offer him hospitality and invite him into her court.

That evening, as they sat together, dining in the great hall, Blodeuedd gazed at her guest and grew to realize that she was wholly in love with him. The emotion that overpowered her rose in Goronwy too, until he also was utterly overcome with love and desire for Blodeuedd.

The Riddle of Lleu's Life

~

Despite the fact that Lleu might return at any time, Goronwy stayed with Blodeuedd for three nights, sleeping together from the first.

They planned how they might continue to live together, and the only way they saw was for Lleu to die. It was left to Blodeuedd to determine how this might be accomplished, for it was known that he was not vulnerable to an ordinary death.

When Lleu returned that very night she feigned affection and, under the pretense of a desire to help him avoid the special circumstances that could slay him, she asked him how he could be slain.

"It would not be easy for me to be killed," he answered. "For only a spear that has been forged for a whole year can mortally wound me. Neither can I be killed indoors nor out of doors, and even then I must neither be on horseback nor on foot, in water or on dry land."

"My lord, this is surpassingly difficult to imagine, I am content that you are indeed safe."

For the ensuing year Goronwy worked on making the spear and, when it was done, Blodeuedd again approached her husband on the subject of his death. Again she feigned concern at the prospect of his demise, and insisted that she would do everything in her power to protect him. But in order to avoid any possibility of disaster, she first needed to know exactly how the circumstances of his death could be brought about.

"My lord, can you show me how you could be killed?"

"I will."

The Wretched Eagle

~

Lleu led her to the bank of a river where a large tub had been set and filled with water, and above it stood a sturdy thatched roof.

Lleu undressed and bathed, for even with some of the special conditions met, he was safe. Then, as he rose to get out, he called for a goat to be brought from the pastures nearby.

As he stood up onto the rim of the tub with the swirling waters lapping at his feet, he set one foot on the back of a goat. In addition to all the other conditions, he was now neither in water nor on dry land.

In that moment which answered the riddle of Lleu's life, Goronwy rose up from his hiding place and pitched the doom-laden spear!

Goronwy's aim was true and the spear pierced Lleu's body. With a shriek that was not quickly lost among the hills, Lleu flew up into the sky as an eagle and ascended out of sight.

Goronwy returned with Blodeuedd to her court, and slept with her that night, and they fondly believed that they had brought their affairs to a successful conclusion. And he established his dominion over the land . . .

The Eagle and the Owl

~

When Gwydyon heard of Lleu's misadventure and betrayal, he set out immediately to discover if the eagle still existed on Earth.

At length his far-ranging journey took him to accept hospitality with the family of a swineherd where there was a strange routine . . .

Early in the morning, as the sty was opened, a sow bolted out so boldly that no one could hold her. Gwydyon followed her as she raced away into a secluded valley. Here she stopped beneath an ancient oak and began to feast on rotten meat that swarmed with maggots.

Gwydyon raised his eyes and saw, perched at the top of the vast canopy, an eagle that dropped down putrid flesh as it fluttered its ragged wings.

Gwydyon sang and coaxed the bird to descend until it perched on his knee. With a touch of his magic wand he transformed Lleu back to his human form, and no one had ever seen a more piteous ruin of a body, barely more than skin and bones!

They returned to Math's court where, over the course of the rest of the year, Lleu was slowly healed and restored to vigor.

Math despatched a host of warriors to accompany Lleu as he rode to challenge Goronwy for the return of his lands.

Gwydyon took a different route and intercepted Blodeuedd as she fled into the mountain. All her maidens were drowned in a treacherous marsh, and eventually she faced him alone.

She had been created from flowers that had basked in the sunshine, but had borne a bitter fruit in the fullness of the season, and now Gwydyon determined that she should be exiled from the light of day, and shunned.

With a stroke of his wand he transformed her into an owl that would endlessly haunt the night. He named her Blodeuwedd in her transformation, which means Flower-Face.

Meanwhile, Lleu had sent his demands for compensation to Goronwy. The usurper offered gold and jewels, and the return of the land, but Lleu rejected them all. He asked only that Goronwy meet him by the river where Lleu had met his doom, and stand there while Lleu aimed a spear at him.

None of Goronwy's company would volunteer to stand in his place, so he was forced to accept the fate that Lleu dictated.

When they met by the river, Goronwy pleaded that he had been misled by a woman and was not wholly responsible. Lleu considered that this might indeed be true, and Goronwy asked that he should be given an element of protection from the spear.

When Lleu accepted this condition, Goronwy seized upon a tall boulder and hid behind it, but Lleu hurled the spear so furiously that it flew straight through the rock and pierced Goronwy's body, breaking his spine so that he was killed.

When Lleu Sure Hand returned to his court he quickly cleared it of Goronwy's influence, and the land happily returned to a time of peace and prosperity.

THE CONQUESTS
OF IRELAND

~

Since its creation, the green and fertile land of
Ireland – the Emerald Isle – has attracted many
people to its shores.

Most are welcome visitors, and may find it
their heart's homeland and choose to stay, but
some arrive in such numbers as to be called
invaders. Wave after wave of these conquerors
have arrived and passed away, sometimes
through natural disasters and other times
through warfare, but each has left a unique
legacy for their successors.

The first people ever to walk the virgin
territory of Ireland were of the tribe of Cessair,
and the tribal chief was a man called Tuan, the
White Ancient. I am that man.

I studied the ancient crafts, and learned the mysteries of the soul and how it finds reincarnation in different forms, including those of animals. I came to understand how to die and how to be reborn, and have practiced this art more times than I can remember — I have been man and beast, sea and sky; I have watched the raising of mighty cities of gold, and have also witnessed their destruction.

Through my many lifetimes I have become the guardian of human courage and dreams.

I am legend incarnate.

I am memory turned myth.

Natural Enemies

~

I, Tuan the White Ancient, dwelt in happiness in Ireland, and my tribe enjoyed peace. But then the Great Flood destroyed us utterly, leaving only me alive.

Living alone and desolate in the ruined fortresses and familiar places now laid waste, I survived for twenty-two years, fending off the attentions of the thriving wolf packs.

Then a new people arrived, led by Partholón, a people who were well cultured and generous. I found a warm welcome in their hearts, and enjoyed the pleasure of their companionship.

Then a plague visited the population, and all perished — all except me, who am both blessed and cursed.

Alone again in the empty fortresses, the rigors of age and solitude took their toll. At length the powerful gray wolves menaced me so that I was forced to desert the fortresses and toil for every scrap of shelter in the forests, all the time aching for human contact. It was the wolves, though, that found me there, and they harried me so closely that I was driven out, and escaped to dwell by the cliffs.

It was from there that I saw the distant sails of a fleet of ships bearing toward the island, driven by a rising wind.

I followed them along the cliff tops, racing for where they might reach land, springing from rock to rock like a wild cat!

As the fleet grew closer, I recognized the markings on their sails: the serpent and the rod. These sailors were from my own tribe!

I paused to drink from a pool of fresh water. And there I caught sight of my reflection. My long years of living as an animal had made strange demands – I was no longer truly human. Naked, I was covered with hair, and with strong, curving nails like claws on my hands and feet — I had become brother to the beasts.

I could not bear to meet my kinsmen like this!

Like a wounded animal I slunk back to my cave. The rising storm shrieked as it smashed against the cliffs yet barely drowned the howls of my broken heart.

And all unheard through the booming thunder, at the foot of the cliffs the fleet was splintered on the rocks, its vessels spilling their cargo of lives into the bloodstained waters . . .

Conann the Conqueror

~

When I awoke it was several days later. To my astonishment I realized that while I slept I had been completely transformed into a stag, fully grown and strong, and with branching antlers that I raised proudly to greet the morning sun!

I sought survivors from the wrecked fleet and found that, from a total of thirty-four ships, nine had made safe landfall.

The chief of this tribe was Nemed, but his dominion over Ireland was not destined to be a peaceful one . . .

Barbarian raiders came from out of the northern blackness. They were the Formor, their skins were as dark as night, and they were ruled by Balor of the Evil Eye, through his warlord – Conann the Conqueror.

In three great battles the tribe of Nemed

met the dark hosts, and I saw that they were victorious.

The Formor rallied again, though, and in the Battle of Conann's Tower, they finally defeated the Nemedians, but so ferocious was the conflict that each side destroyed the other.

I watched as the straggling remnants of the Formor fled to Africa. Those of the Nemedians left alive scattered to the corners of the Earth. Of these, it was Nemed's son Fergus the Half-Red, who sailed across the narrow sea to a new land, that he named in honor of his son: Britain.

Dark Rumors and Nightmares

~

When I had grown old and tired once more, again I slept my magical sleep. I awakened with the vigor of youth pounding through my veins – before, I had known the grace and pride of the noble stag; now I, Tuan, thrilled with the fierce power of the tusked black boar.

From my vantage point in the undergrowth I espied that newcomers had settled in Ireland. These were the Fir Bolg, descendants of those Nemedians who had been defeated at the Battle of the Tower of Conann, and who had eventually wandered as far abroad as Greece.

Although they grew prosperous in the fertile land, bloodcurdling rumors crawled through their minds. Balor of the Evil Eye, ruler of the dark-skinned Formor, was whispered to be amassing a fleet so large it would mantle the entire western ocean in a shroud of green and black sails. There was no doubt but that they would be defenseless against such an enemy!

Even the noble Eochaí, king of the Fir Bolg, fell victim to nightmares. From the western ocean he saw arise a flock of birds that flew like a black veil across the sky. They descended on his people with beaks slashing like scythes, until only lumps of carrion were left like a viscous red tide around a mountainous island of skulls, where the birds roosted after feasting.

The court wizard, César, rightly interpreted this dream as a warning of impending doom — although not at the hands of the Formor . . .

The Tuatha Dé Danann

~

I grew old again while the doom-laden omens drew a somber pall over the lives of the Fir Bolg.

When I awoke from my magical sleep my spirit soared into the fresh blue sky, dancing with the golden clouds of dawn. To my surprise and delight I had become a sea-eagle, lord of the skies!

On the eve of Beltane, sacred feast of the sun god Bel, eerie vapors arose from the lakes and mingled with the low gray clouds that covered the sky. The people of the Fir Bolg were locked in a gloom that stabbed to their very hearts.

I, Tuan the White Ancient, alone could pierce the veil and I flew powerfully upward, through the thick dark clouds, and out into the bright light of the sun.

There I beheld, with awe and wonder, a

great fleet of ships that sailed the wind, with the billowing clouds breaking beneath their prows like the waves of the sea!

With sails blazoned with ravens, and colorful banners flying high with pride that sang of heroic deeds and high magic, the fleet of the Tuatha Dé Danann rode through the skies above Ireland.

A Bond of Friendship

~

A thousand heroes and countless followers were borne on those enchanted ships, and peerless among them stood a flame-haired giant of a man – Nuada, their king. All were descendants of Nemed: once scattered after the Battle of Conann's Tower, they had now returned to their ancestral homeland.

With them they brought four ancient treasures: the sacred Stone of Destiny, the Sword of Light, the Spear of Victory, and the wondrous Caldron of the Dagda.

As I circled high above them, watching the sunlight glitter on their shields and spear points, I also saw among their company three sisters – Macha, Mórrigan and Neman – war witches called, together, the Badb, and renowned as much for their grisly appetites as for their seductive loveliness.

The host disembarked among the Red Hills of Rein, in Connaught, and quickly established a fortress surrounded by strong ramparts.

When word of this new settlement reached Eochaí at his great hall at Tara, he despatched their champion warrior to seek out the strangers and discover their intentions.

When Nuada of the Tuatha Dé Danann saw the lone warrior standing before their gates, he sent his own champion to hear what he had to say.

The two warriors lowered their shields and inspected each other's spears: those of the Fir Bolg were broad-tipped and heavy, while those of the Tuatha Dé Danann were slim and sharply pointed, and both men appreciated the terrible wounds such weapons could inflict.

Each told the other of their history and, when they realized they were both of

Nemed's lineage, they embraced as brothers, swearing an oath of friendship.

The Fir Bolg champion voiced his heartfelt hope that the two tribes would share the land of Ireland in peace and prosperity.

The champion of the Tuatha Dé Danann declared that king Nuada wished for nothing more. "But," he added, "King Nuada will settle for nothing less, and will take half of Ireland as his share of the birthright — by force of arms if needs be."

Although joyful at their newfound friendship, the champions each returned to his own tribe with heart full of foreboding, for they both fully realised that few kings give up half their kingdom simply for the asking . . .

Dark Forces Gather

~

Eochaí, king of the Fir Bolg, saw in the host that had landed on the west of Ireland the image of the dark invaders of his dream. And although he knew it would cause a terrible war, he could not surrender half his kingdom.

When no words of friendship came from the Fir Bolg king, Nuada led the Tuatha Dé Danann to a stronger defensive position, against the flank of the Black Hill, Belgatan. There they dug unassailable earthworks and raised a mighty fortress.

The Fir Bolg themselves were not idle but were mustering armies from every part of Ireland, assembling them all at the royal court of Tara, making ready for the day when their king and warlord Eochaí would lead them forth to liberate their kingdom from the invaders.

As I circled high in the air, I watched the massing of men, and listened to the lament of the women as they gave up their loved ones to the fierce embrace of war.

Then, as the clouds gathered together, shouldering out the clear blue sky, I heard the songbirds of Tara fall silent. I saw them all hurry for their hiding places and cower with fright.

Then, as I flew through the deep darkness, I saw the Badb – the three warrior witches – brewing a spell of doom in the air . . .

The Battle of Witchcraft and Wizardry

~

Through the unnatural silence rose a low moan, as if from the very Earth itself. As it rose in volume it also rose in pitch, until it was clear that it issued from the ancient standing stones that ringed the plain of Tara.

Inexorably the sounds crescendoed into the shrieking wail of the Banshee!

Worse was to come though, for the cry was rousing the wraiths of the dead from their long slumber, and drawing them into the midst of the Fir Bolg camp. And, as if the appearance of these phantoms wasn't bad enough, the Badb also summoned a legion of winged specters that writhed and fought in the air above the stricken host of mortal warriors.

All the while the shrill cry of the Banshee was accompanied by the booming thunder that followed the violent flashes of tree-splintering forked lightning.

Then the sorcerous Badb conjured Carnún, the Horned God, to preside over the reign of terror. He came as a huge serpentine dragon with glaring red eyes, and wherever his shadow fell there also fell a fine rain of blood, drenching the Fir Bolg encampment.

Eochaí their king summoned his chief wizard, César, and commanded him to counter this supernatural attack. The wizard had been reluctant to involve himself in the fray as he knew well that the Badb were more powerful than he, but now he had no choice.

It was to the great stone of Tara that César went, grimly resolved to call forth whatever forces were necessary to aid the terrified Fir Bolg. Drenched by the rain of blood, deafened by the screeching Banshee, and surrounded by the vicious spears of deadly lightning, César stood alone.

For three days he worked to conjure all

the powers at his disposal, weaving his wizardry into the wind, the water, and the very earth. And by the night of the third day he had won a small circle of ground where no blood rained, where no wraiths walked, and where no wind vied to tear the breath from his body.

Here he exhausted every possibility of turning the tide of this magical war against the Badb – all except one. Faced with the continuing onslaught, César grimly resolved to take a terrible and irrevocable step. To save his people he would turn to the elder god from beyond the stars whom the Fir Bolg had long since abandoned: Crom-Crúach.

Within his circle, magically separate from the swirling chaos that still engulfed royal Tara, César burned sigils and ogham runes into the turf. These he painted blue with woad, red with goat's blood, and white with chalk. He lit nine candles while he incanted the words of the dead language that Crom-Crúach understands.

An eerie green glow began permeating the air above the plain of Tara. As it grew brighter the shrill howl from the stones was quieted and the specters and wraiths swept out of the sky to return to their secret abodes.

As the green light grew brighter still, hanging in the air, the rain of blood ceased as the great dragon Carnún glided away to hide in the dark recesses of the earth.

Then the strange luminosity blazed into a ball of blinding green light that spun through the air above the plain of Tara. Under this unnatural sun the Great Worm Crom-Crúach writhed out of the black smoke that gushed from the candles in the circle, where César stood in bitter triumph.

He had swept the unholy hordes of the Badb from the skies above the Fir Bolg host, but César knew, as I know, that the elder gods do not answer the calls of mortal men without exacting a price. César owed the elder god a great debt, a debt that Crom-Crúach would not forget . . .

For now though, the Fir Bolg were freed from the three days and nights of dread and terror, and they lost no more time in preparing to march upon the fortress of the Tuatha Dé Danann.

A Deadly Game

～

I, Tuan, was once chieftain of the people of Cessair, and I know the hard choices that send loved ones into the fire of battle. Transparent to me was the mind of Nuada, chief of the Tuatha Dé Danann.

He had led his people through wearying and painful years of traveling. From Greece they had been ousted by the Assyrians, and had taken refuge in Scythia. There they found a corrupt government, and chose not to stay. They even traveled as far as Hyperborea, where they sojourned for seven years in the realm beyond the North Wind. And then they returned to their ancestral homeland of Ireland.

Nuada had now visited the sacred Mountain of Nemed and communed with the spirits of his ancestors and, even if it meant a terrible battle, he was committed to settling his people here.

He gave orders both that the smiths prepare plenty of weapons, and that the physicians prepare healing baths.

He advised that the warriors be grouped together according to their clans, with parents side by side with their children. In this way, not only could the youths learn from the veterans, but Nuada knew that no father will see his son slain while he yet has the strength to prevent the slaying.

Even so, when the Fir Bolg armies were close by, he sent messengers again to propose peace between the camps. But to no avail: Eochaí still refused to partition the land.

Despite the painstaking activity of making ready for war, many young warriors grew hot-blooded and impatient. The Fir Bolg challenged the Tuatha Dé Danann to a sporting contest – hurling – a game of skill and strength.

The challenge was accepted and the game

began, but as soon as the Tuatha Dé Danann had scored once, the Fir Bolg turned their hurling sticks upon them – and routed their opponents, leaving many young players dead or dying on the field of play.

Many oaths of vengeance were made that night in the fortress of the Tuatha Dé Danann.

The First Battle

~

On Midsummer's morning the Tuatha Dé Danann marched out of their fortress beating their shields with swords, spears and axes, and yelling war cries that were barely heard over the braying of the horns of war.

And through their midst wheeled the three witches of the Badb, gowned in black with crimson veils, with torches in their hands that belched black smoke.

The Fir Bolg approached in silence until a contingent of giant men from the hills, naked save for their war paint, broke to the fore – howling with hatred.

As the sides grew closer each fully realized that no easy victory was possible. Then all such thoughts were drowned in the roar of battle.

I watched the meeting of these hosts, and saw the carnage in its entirety. At first

Dagda, a mighty champion, drove back the wild men of the hills, but his force was outflanked, and the Fir Bolg loosed a tide of blood from the bodies of the Tuatha Dé Danann.

After the rout, each warrior of the victorious army took a stone and a severed head from the battlefield, to heap up a cairn in sight of Eochaí their king. And he was satisfied.

The Unknown Warrior

~

Before the next day's battle began, Eochaí bathed in his healing well. Its waters were thick and green with potent herbs.

Alone and unarmed he saw the sky suddenly darken, and out of the shadows stepped three fully armed warriors.

They went to strike him dead as he stood there, but a ray of sunlight burst through the sinister clouds and there appeared before him a warrior with weapons shining with a pure radiance.

The four warriors fought until none remained alive – but the king was saved.

Eochaí ordered that a cairn of white stones, in honor of his heroism, should be raised over the corpse of his unknown champion.

The Red Tide of War

~

I watched the second day of battle ebb and flow its bloody tide across the plain where once I, Tuan the stag, had led my herd in peace.

The Tuatha Dé Danann won the day, though but barely, but still the Fir Bolg took their grisly trophies from the field as they retreated back to where Eochaí awaited their news.

On the fourth day Dagda set up tall pillars of wood and stone in the middle of the plain, and there he positioned his strongest warriors.

His plan was simple and effective: he drove the hordes of the unwitting Fir Bolg toward the pillars, each of which was guarded by a hero.

The Fir Bolg warriors found that they dared not strike sweeping blows at these sentries lest their blades be broken on the stones and stout wooden posts. The advantage lay with the Tuatha Dé Danann, and they won the day handsomely, although not without sickening loss of life.

That evening the Tuatha Dé Danann followed the Fir Bolg's example, and brought heads and stones back from the battlefield. And, in their own fortress, they raised a cairn of their enemy's dead in a grim gesture of triumph.

A Word to the Wise

~

That night, Mórrigan of the Badb flew through the moonlight in raven's form, and settled on the gruesome cairn in the Tuatha Dé Danann camp. Then, in the form of a beautiful maiden, she slipped into Nuada's tent . . .

Through the night they lay together in the hot embrace of love and life while, outside, countless fallen warriors lay locked in the grip of death.

When at last he slept, Nuada dreamed in the embrace of the Mórrigan.

Love, death and dreams, these are fabric of legend. And as Nuada traveled the paths of his dreaming his journey took him to the earliest time, when beauty alone was the measure of achievements.

Then he traveled closer in time and saw, as I have seen, the building and destruction of many mighty cities. He too saw the battle of Conann's Tower, and he heard prophesied his own role in bringing the people of Nemed back to Ireland.

The next moment he saw a vision of tomorrow, of the fresh dead that would lie slaughtered on the field of battle. Each corpse turned its head and faced him, crying, "No more!"

The same words were on his lips as Nuada awoke.

"Your witchcraft, Mórrigan, must staunch this bloodshed!"

The Battle of Blood and Magic

~

On the fourth, and final, day of battle both kings joined the fray.

Nuada strapped himself to a pillar of stone to protect his back and was surrounded by his Scythian bodyguard, while Eochaí was circled around by thirteen brothers whose battle skills were famed throughout the land.

As the tightly massed armies collided once more in a fury of sharp blades and splintering bone, the Fir Bolg sought to push toward Nuada, intent on killing the king.

As the fighting grew close to him a raven swooped down and alighted on the top of the pillar. With the voice of Mórrigan it told Nuada to fling his round shield up after the bird as it flew aloft.

The raven took off at once, quickly rising high in the blue sky, and with a mighty effort

Nuada hurled the shield up after the shrinking black shape. The shield, though, did not appear to grow smaller the further it went, and neither did it fall back down to Earth.

Such was Mórrigan's magic that the shield covered the sun, blotting out the light across the entire field of battle!

Out of this darkness rode the Badb in blazing chariots at the head of a phantom army of nightmare creatures that filled the sky with horror and the hearts of the Fir Bolg with dread. The Banshee shrieks of the supernatural host tore maddeningly through the magic-darkened day.

As the Badb wheeled around above the enemy host many men were burned by the fire that dripped and spat as the sisters brandished their black, smoking torches.

César, the Fir Bolg wizard, knew of only one way to counter the witchcraft of the threefold Badb, only one way to banish their unnatural army and release the Fir Bolg warriors from the grip of sorcery.

He called once again on the name of the elder god Crom-Crúach . . .

The Wrath of Crom-Crúach

~

Amid the chaos of slaughter I alone witnessed the coming, not of Crom-Crúach himself, but of his close kin and emissary.

Almost insignificant at first, rising out of the smoking darkness, the pallor of white bone arrested my gaze. Growing larger by the moment, I saw horns upon the gleaming dome of its skull although the rest of this living skeleton was human enough.

I, Tuan, watched as it clawed at the creatures conjured by the Badb, slashing them out of the air. And all the while it was growing bigger and more powerful.

The Badb had faced this monster once before, in the time of Nemed himself, and knew they were powerless to resist its primeval lust for death. As they fled the field the mind-numbing wailing died on a gust of

spirit wind, and the Fir Bolg rallied their
courage.

Nuada faced this skeletal creature that
now loomed as large as the sky. With his
spirit blazing and his battle frenzy at full
pitch, Nuada turned his grip on his sword
and sent it singing through the silent air as a
spear on a mission of death.

It struck and pierced the skull between the
eyes and the horns, and the wailing of the
Badb's terrible legion was as song compared
to the sounds that agony ripped from that
skeletal throat!

While men stood stunned the monstrous
figure of animated bone turned and dove
away through the churning magic-wrought
vapors that hung heavy in the sky.

As the mortal battle resumed I saw the Fir
Bolg wizard César realize the price of this
defeat.

In the magic circle, in front of the
standing stone carved with the runes of

ancient magic, he stood, paralyzed by the sight of the faint green glow that limned the monolith.

Crom-Crúach had sent his emissary to collect the souls of the vanquished to join him in his infernal realm. But César had underestimated the Tuatha Dé Danann: their mortal prowess had broken the power of the ancient gods, and such humiliation would not be borne lightly.

As the green light brightened sickeningly, César sought to quit the circle of sigils he had traced on the ground. But not for all his strength nor petitions to the new gods that had turned the minds of men away from allegiance to their primitive forebears, not for the sake of his very life could he leave that blighted spot.

The light burned brighter so that not even I, Tuan the sea-eagle, could stare into its fierce green heart.

When, at last, it faded into darkness the

Fir Bolg saw with horror that it had taken
César along with it, body and soul . . .

The Death of a King

~

With renewed vigor the Fir Bolg warriors sought to attack the pillar where Nuada held his ground.

Their might beat down all before them until their champion who had first spoken with the Tuatha Dé Danann, and had hoped for peace between the tribes, faced the king in single combat.

The fight was fierce but Nuada had been weakened by his battle against the infernal prince, and in a momentary error he let his opponent through his guard.

This lapse of strength cost him dearly: with a crashing blow his foe's sword crashed through his shield and severed his right arm.

His companions leaped into the arena to prevent a further mortal blow, but allowed the Fir Bolg champion to escape.

Meanwhile, Eochaí the Fir Bolg leader,

had fared scarcely better. Although he had escaped any serious wounds, he had realized that his forces were spent and the war was all but lost. A victim of sheer fatigue, he left the field of battle a broken man.

His son Sláine engaged Nuada's son Lughaí in combat but these two youths had lost the will to inflict any more agonising deaths on the opposing side. In prospect of the peace to come they withdrew the men under their personal control and, as part of a mutually agreed truce, neither took further part in the conflict.

The three other sons of Nuada harried the Fir Bolg king, Eochaí, until, with his back to the sea, he met them in fierce fight, and all four perished

The Future of a Nation

~

Without their king to command them, the Fir Bolg held a council to decide whether to fight on, negotiate the surrender of a part of Ireland, or leave the country in self-imposed exile.

Although the Fir Bolg champion again advised the partition of the land, the council voted against him.

That night, the remaining few hundreds of the countless thousands that had boldly begun this war stole up to the very gates of the fortress of the Tuatha Dé Danann.

Seizing the element of surprise they quickly burst through and ran riot through the night.

When the wakened sentinels eventually held them in check, the Fir Bolg champion challenged Nuada to finish the duel they had begun the day before.

Although perilously weak from his injury, Nuada accepted the challenge — asking only that his opponent should bind his sword arm, so that the fight be fair.

Realizing the extent of Nuada's wounds, Streng, the Fir Bolg champion, lost heart for the killing of yet another brave warrior. Instead he suggested that their duel had already reached its natural end.

Recognizing the stature of a man who could so easily have killed their king yet whose heart overcame the natural call for vengeance, the Tuatha Dé Danann generously awarded him and his people a place in the future of Ireland.

Streng was painfully aware that if Eochaí had agreed to give half of the country to their newly arrived kinsfolk, as he had advised, none of this mutual destruction would have taken place.

He chose Connaught which, whilst not equal to half the kingdom, was the best he could hope for in view of the fact that the Fir Bolg had very nearly lost everything in their desire to keep it all to themselves!

The Future Past . . .

~

Down through the years the battlefield cairns and pillars of those bloodthirsty days remain as mute testimony to the valor of men that test the will of fate.

Nuada, whilst victorious, was barred by custom from ruling his tribe, for his mutilation was unseemly for a king. His champion, Breas, who had first met the Fir Bolg and agreed that peace was the best option, took his place at the head of his people.

Until, that is, Nuada was fitted with an arm of silver that moved as well as any limb of flesh and blood. Thereafter Nuada resumed his rightful place, and ruled wisely, and his people prospered.

They fared so well that when the Formor sought to rise up against them from across the western sea, planning to sweep like a dark wind over the land of Ireland, Nuada and his people withstood them valiantly.

In the battle, though, I, Tuan, saw Nuada fall into death at the hand of Balor of the Evil Eye. But neither did Balor survive that battle.

The Tuatha Dé Danann defeated the Formor once and for all time, and they and their descendants enjoyed, for many a joyful generation, the fertile bounty of Ireland, the country they call the Emerald Isle.

All this I witnessed as I grew old. And I have now told my story, for I was once more born as a man.

Where next I shall be born I cannot but wonder, and then what sights shall I see!

But none shall know my story until I speak again with the voice you understand.

I am Tuan.

I am memory become myth.

THE DESTRUCTION OF DA DERGA'S HOSTEL

~

Sometimes a child is born with a bright and valiant destiny to fulfil; others are born with a doom that will inevitably catch up with them and overtake them, sweeping away also anyone else who is close at the time.

Conare, though born into the family of a king, and enjoying both excellent physique and an exquisite mind, lived his life under sentence of several gessa (or taboos). Breaking these would be the true cause of his death . . .

The king of Temuir was Eterscélae, and he was barren. A prophesy had foretold, however, that he would have an heir born of a woman of unknown ancestry.

When news came to his ears that such a

woman, reputed, moreover, to be of surpassing beauty, was being kept in seclusion by a foster family, she was sent for at once.

The foster family was that of a herdsman, and they had found the girl as a baby in a kennel, nuzzling among pups at the teats of their hound bitch. They had reared her tenderly but, because of her great beauty, they feared for the preservation of her honor, and wove around her a house without a door, but only a small window through which they could pass food and other supplies, and a skylight.

There the maiden Mess Búachalla passed her days engaged in embroidery, a skill at which she soon excelled.

One night a bird flew in at the skylight and, standing in the middle of the floor, shuffled off the robe of its feathers, and spoke to her.

"Tomorrow, the king's men will come and demolish your house and take you by force to be with the king. But you will not go alone, for you *will be with child, our child, and his name shall be Conare. And he must never kill a bird."*

The Feast of the Bull

~

Conare was raised as the king's son and heir and, after the custom of the day, was fostered.

He had been born with three great gifts: the gift of hearing, of seeing, and of judgment. He was raised with three foster brothers who were the sons of Dond Désa, a champion of a band of roving warriors. Conare taught one of his gifts to each of them.

As they grew, these four dressed the same, rode identical horses, and went everywhere and did everything together.

When king Eterscélae died, there was a great gathering for the naming of the new king, which would be accomplished at the Feast of the Bull.

During this sacred ceremony a bull was slain and cooked, and one man would eat as much of the bull's flesh and drink of its broth as much as he could stomach. Then this man would sleep and in his dreams he would see the future king – the dreamer would perish if he failed to report his visions accurately!

The four young men had been invited to attend the Feast, but had spent most of the time chariot racing together instead. Finally though, Conare left his foster brothers and went off alone.

Conare's Bird Clan

~

A flock of huge, speckled birds caught his eye
and he turned to pursue them. They fled
ahead of him, always staying just further
away than he could cast his spear. At length
his horses grew weary, and Conare leaped
down and followed on foot, taking his sling
with him.

Even when they came to the ocean the
birds did not stop, and Conare took to the
wave after them.

Then the flock shuffled off their robes of
feathers, and turned to face him,
brandishing swords and spears!

One among the flock addressed Conare,
saying, "I am king of your father bird clan,
and these are all your kin. Now, you should
go to the Feast of the Bull tonight, go just as
you are: with a stone in your sling, and
naked.

"If you do this you will be richly rewarded and peerless among men, yet you must accept the price, which is that you will be subject to certain gessa, restrictions on your freedom that, once broken, will magically hasten your doom.

"You must not travel following your right hand around Temuir, nor following your left around Brega; nor hunt the beasts of Cernae; nor leave Temuir every ninth night; nor spend the night where firelight is seen from within or without; nor be preceded by three Deirgs into the house of Deirg; nor allow plundering under your reign; nor allow a single man or woman into your abode after dusk; nor meddle in a dispute between your servants."

Impressed by these strange tidings, and thinking the gessa manageable, Conare did as he was advised.

Conare Becomes King

~

It was dawn by the time Conare reached his destination in Temuir. At the entrance to the Feast stood men with robes fit to garb a king. And they instantly clothed Conare in this costly apparel, for he was the living image of the new king that the dreaming had foretold.

From the first day of his reign there was peace and prosperity in Ireland. Even the weather was pacified: no thunder was heard in Conare's kingdom!

But his foster brothers were discontent. Their father had led a life of plundering, and such they had reckoned would be their own destiny – except that plundering was now outlawed to protect Conare from breaking this geiss (taboo).

Secretly they tested his position by plundering one pig, one calf and one cow from a farmer. The farmer complained to Conare who, through his gifts, recognized the culprits. Unwilling to punish his childhood friends himself, he instructed the farmer to approach them directly.

But when the farmer challenged the sons for following in the ways of their father, he barely escaped with his life!

Being afraid to trouble the king further, the farmer accepted his losses. But the very next year the same events recurred, with the same results.

And so it continued until the three plunderers grew so bold as to muster themselves into a band of one hundred and fifty bloodthirsty warriors.

Conare's Judgment

~

Unable yet again to properly punish his friends from youth, Conare decided to equip them as a fully-fledged raiding party and send them to plunder across the sea, in Britain.

And with their leaving, complete and prosperous peace descended on Ireland once more.

At length though, Conare's attention was diverted by the rumour of a war brewing between two more of his childhood friends.

He left his court to negotiate a truce between them, and he used his renowned judgment to bring a successful end to this effort. In the process however, he broke his geiss against meddling in just such a dispute . . .

Having been away for ten days and, thereby, broken another geiss, as he returned to Temuir he encountered lands burned to ashes and witnessed the grief and panic of people whose communities had been raided for plunder.

In Britain his foster brothers had met and allied themselves with Ingcél Cáech, the son of a king whose fierce ambition had led him to murder his father, mother and his own seven brothers, all in a single night.

Once the partners had pillaged Britain they turned, as their pact demanded, to plunder Ireland. And the scenes of devastation that Conare encountered were all of their doing.

With the breaking of these gessa, Conare's life began to spiral inexorably out of control . . .

The Hostel of Destruction

~

Forced by the warlike actions that they had run into, Conare's company wheeled to the right hand around Temuir, and to the left around Brega; and they hunted for food in Cernae.

As these strict gessa gave way before the urgent needs of the moment, Conare was exiled by the spirits of his ancestors.

No such person can expect to thrive, and a terrible fear entered Conare's heart.

That night they determined to lodge at Da Derga's hostel, the only safe haven within reach, yet it was also the house of Deirg. It was a massive building with seven entrances, and seven suites between each entrance, yet there was only one door, and this door moved according to the direction of the wind.

Ahead of Conare rode three men, all

attired in red — even their weapons, horses and teeth were of the same unearthly hue. These were three Deirgs who, despite entreaties, would not turn aside from entering the hostel before the king. With the breaking of yet another geiss, Conare realized that this hostel would be no safe haven after all.

His conviction was confirmed when a single man whom they passed on the road pledged to bring him, after dark, a boar upon which to feast.

Even as Conare settled down in his apartment at the hostel, shortly after sunset, a single woman came to claim hospitality of him.

Mindful of his geiss, Conare sought to dissuade her with gifts aplenty.

She stood leaning on the doorpost, and her mouth was set on one side of her face, and her beard reached her shoes, and she cast a baleful glare over the company.

"I see," she gloated, "that none of you will leave this place except as a morsel carried aloft in the claws of a carrion bird!"

Then she declared her supernatural kinship with the Badb, warrior witches who gather to feast at the scene of martial slaughter.

Realising clearly that she had come to oversee his doom, Conare relented in despair rather than be dishonored by refusing a woman his hospitality.

The Plunderers Scent Prey

Ingcél had grown impatient of waiting to seize a major prize, one the equal to that which he had shared with his Irish partners when they worked together in Britain. Their combined forces totaled some fifty thousand warriors.

Spies with the gifts of seeing and hearing were despatched to find the choicest target.

The royal hostel of Da Derga was an obvious place to look, and it was not neglected. Neither was it difficult to see because the hosteler was roasting boar for the evening feast, and the light from the cooking fires poured out of the seven entrances.

The spy with the gift of hearing reported that the horses and men of a great king were residing within that night. The spy with the gift of seeing recognized the retinue as that of king Conare.

When Ingcél heard the information he asked what manner of king was Conare. One of the foster brothers who had once been so close to Conare answered that his reign was good, peaceful, the weather was clement and guaranteed a fruitful harvest, and even the wolves confined their attentions to wild game, taking just one bull calf from each farmer's enclosure each year.

"In Conare's reign," he summed up, "we have all of the three crowns of Ireland: the crown of wheat, the crown of flowers, and the crown of acorns. It would be grievous to destroy such a king."

"Such a destruction," answered Ingcél, "would equal the one I shared with you in my own country. I will go and see for myself before settling our plans."

Ingcél had only one eye, yet it had three pupils. He used part of it to cast a baleful glare over the hostel as he peered through the wheels of the seventeen chariots that were parked outside every entrance.

At length though, he was spotted by guards in the hostel and forced to flee into the night.

When he returned to the plunderer's encampment he sat with his five other commanders, a party that included all three of Conare's foster brothers. And these were surrounded by concentric circles of the company, all intently listening to the council.

"Whether or not king Conare is present in the hostel," he declared, "the hostel is full of riches tonight. It will repay me handsomely for the booty I shared with you in my native Britain."

The Roll of Heroes in the Hostel

~

"It is your right," said Fer Rogain, one of the foster brothers of Conare, sadly, "to sack the hostel, but tell us of the people you saw within."

"Opposite the king sat a warrior in whose hands I saw a sword with a gold hilt, and a spear with five points. And with him were nine men who could take their ivory handled swords by the point, twist them around and when they let go, the metal blades would spring back straight again."

Fer Rogain knew the prowess of every hero in Ireland and summed up their abilities for the council. This warrior he named as Cormac Cond Longes, the very best fighter in the land, capable of slaying ninety men and still evading death at the end of a battle.

Lomnae Drúth, one of the six in the

council and another son of Dond Désa, cried, "Grief to him who executes this destruction of Da Derga's hostel, even if it is only for the sake of this one man. If I ruled this council I would turn away from this place, if only for the goodness and honor of this one man."

"You do not rule this council," chided Ingcél, "and there will be clouds of blood!"

Then Ingcél continued his account of his spying expedition: "I saw another apartment in which there were three enormous brown men whose hair hung equally long in front of their faces as it did behind their heads, and all their clothes and weapons were black."

Again Fer Rogain named these men and described their great prowess in battle, and again Lomnae Drúth pleaded on their behalf to prevent their destruction.

"Then I saw another apartment with nine men, handsome and with yellow hair, and each had a four-toned pipe."

"These," said Fer Rogain, "are the best pipers in the world, they are also battle hardened veterans, and fighting them is as hard as fighting shadows for they are supernatural beings."

"Then I saw a man with bristling hair so long and sharp that if a sack of apples were tipped over him each would be skewered and none fall to the floor!

"Then I saw a room with three huge men, and in that room was a shield with a sharp edge of serrated iron, and with a central boss as bulbous as a caldron that could cook four pigs with room for four oxen on top! There was also a sword fully thirty feet long and such sparks flew from it that the room was brightly lit up. And there too I saw two lakes beside a mountain, and two stretched ox hides beside an oak. Explain this."

"This," said Fer Rogain, "is Conare's champion, Macc Cécht. The lakes are his eyes, and the mountain his nose, the hides are his ears and the oak is the hair on his head. He can slay six hundred men without pausing for rest. As incalculable as hailstones or stars in the sky will be the broken skulls of our company before he is finished, and even then he will not be slain."

At these grim tidings the entire company of plunderers retreated over the crests of three more ridges further away from the hostel.

"Then," continued Ingcél, "I saw three youths, fair of feature and voice, and their long hair would rise up to float above their ears every time their eyes would open. Explain this."

Fer Rogain said nothing, but wept fully one third of the night. "These," he said when he had regained his voice, "are Conare's sons."

"Grief to him who proceeds with this destruction, if only for the sakes of these three excellent youths!" cried Lomnae Drúth.

"You do not rule here." warned Ingcél. "Bloody clouds engulf you!"

Then he continued his account: "Next, I saw a room with three misshapen men, as if the sea had formed their features. They had three rows of teeth that extend from ear to ear. Explain that."

"These," said Fer Rogain, "are hostages held so that the Formor do not afflict our lives with their magic. Although they may not bear arms here, they can each slay two hundred men with their bare hands without pausing."

"Then I saw three men with limbs as stout as a man's waist. They tossed their swords up in the air, and then the scabbards, and the swords returned to their hands already sheathed.

"Then I saw the most handsome warrior in all Ireland, clad in a crimson cloak. One of his eyes was blue, the other black; one cheek white, the other speckled like a foxglove; and his hair was so like a ram's fleece that if a sack of red nuts were spilled over it, none would fall to the floor."

"This," said Fer Rogain, "is Conall Cernach, the man most like Conare himself, and they are great friends. He will engage us at each and every one of the hostel's seven entrances, and three hundred of our company will he slay without pause."

"Then in the most richly decorated apartment I have seen, I saw three men. The young man in the middle, with gray-blue eyes and yellow hair, was the most beautiful I have ever seen, and had the prowess of a lord and the insight of a seer: a man who rules as much by his own right as by the will of his people.

"His cloak had the appearance of the first mist of summer, yet it changed hue constantly, with ever increasing beauty.

Upon his breast was a disc of gold that stretched from his chin to his navel. And many jewels adorned his body, including one that shone like the full moon. Explain this."

"These," said Fer Rogain, "are two companions who will not stray more than a foot from their lord in battle. And the man between them is Conare. This king is the most powerful yet most gentle king in the world, there is no defect in him, neither in his physique nor his dignity.

"Six hundred men will be slain before he collects his weapons, and as many thereafter without a pause. If he leaves the hostel he will pursue you far and wide, but he may be prevented from leaving by an overwhelming thirst."

"Grief to him who carries through this plan of destruction!" cried Lomnae Drúth.

"You are not in charge." countered Ingcél. "Clouds of blood will engulf you!

"Then I saw a circle of twelve brightly

clad men with yellow hair guarding Conare.

"Then I saw a freckled boy in a red cloak, sitting in the center of the hostel, weeping. His hair was of three colors: green, orange and gold, and around him sat one hundred and fifty other lads, each armed with a thorn spike atop a reed. I felt one of my pupils being blinded. Explain this."

"This boy," said Fer Rogain, weeping tears of blood, "is the doomed son of Conare. He is seven years of age and Lé Fer Flaith by name, and the boys around him are his special court."

"Grief to him who proceeds with this destruction, if only for the sake of this child!" cried Lomnae Drúth.

"You do not govern here," warned Ingcél. "Bloody clouds engulf you!"

Then he continued his account: "In front of that apartment, I saw six men with tin brooches on their green cloaks, and they could wrap each other in their cloaks so swiftly that the eye could not see the movement.

"There too I saw a man with white hair and a cloak of all colors. I watched him cast up nine iron swords, nine silver shields and nine gold apples, leaving only one in his hand. And although these things swarmed around him like bees, none fell to the ground. Yet as I watched, his trick collapsed around his feet and he said, 'I am watched by the baleful eye of a man with three pupils, and grievous is the meaning of this. Check the entrance!' A man ran this errand and returned saying that the sons of Dond Désa, foster brothers to Conare, had renounced their grudge against him. Explain this."

"The trickster is the wise fool and bard who entertains king Conare. His prowess in battle is also considerable, and although wounded, he will escape alive."

"Grief to him who proceeds with this destruction, happy would be the man to spare this glad entertainer," cried Lomnae Drúth.

"You do not rule here," warned Ingcél. "Bloody clouds engulf you!"

Then he continued his account: "Next, before the same suite, I saw nine men wearing short trousers, each bore a shield and a sword with an ivory handle.

"Then, in another apartment, I saw two men who rushed around each other so swiftly I could barely see them.

"Then, in the suite next to the king's, I saw three chiefs with graying hair. Their limbs were thick as a man's waist, and each bore a black sword that could split a hair floating on water. The chief between the others held a mighty lance, whose shaft would be a full load for an ox team to pull. From its point, secured by fifty rivets, sparks erupted. Then he thrice smote his palm with its butt, and plunged the point into the dark liquid that bubbled and spat in a caldron large enough to seethe a bullock. I watched and saw that if the sparks were not quenched quickly then flames would erupt and threaten to set a blaze in the hostel. Explain this."

"This lance," said Fer Rogain, "is a wonder that was found at the battle of Mag Tured, and such is its power that it can sense when it will soon loose floods of enemy blood, and at such times it will spout bursts of flame unless it is continually quenched in a caldron of venom. Even pointing the lance at an enemy will slay him outright and, if thrown, this lance will slay nine men, and one will be a king, a prince, or a plundering chieftain."

"Grief to him who proceeds with this destruction, if only for the sakes of him who wields this wondrous weapon!" cried Lomnae Drúth.

"You do not rule here," warned Ingcél. "Bloody clouds engulf you!"

Then Ingcél continued his account: "Next, I saw an apartment with three powerful men, men whom few would choose to stare at for fear of their reaction. Apart from their swords they each had an iron flail, and each had seven chains twisted into three strands, and at the end of each strand was an enormous chunk of metal. They also each bore an iron staff of metal with nine chains that had a further rod of iron similar in size and weight to the staff itself.

"Then I saw in another suite a man flanked by lads, one as fair as the other was dark, and the man himself had flame-red hair and ruddy cheeks, and his eyes were blue. He had an ivory-hilted sword and wore a white tunic with red embroidery, and a green cloak. And he was busy catering to all the apartments of the hostel. Explain this."

"This man," said Fer Rogain. "Is Da Derga, the hosteler, and the lads are his foster sons."

"Grief to him who proceeds with this destruction, if only for the sakes of these this excellent man and the two children!" cried Lomnae Drúth.

"You do not rule here," warned Ingcél. "Bloody clouds engulf you!"

Then he continued his account: "Next, I saw a suite with three men, who were red all over, even to their teeth. Explain this."

"These," said Fer Rogain, "are three supernatural beings whom you cannot wound, but neither will they wound any of our company: they were sentenced to suffer three destructions and this, the destruction of Da Derga's hostel, is the last of their punishments."

Then Ingcél continued his account: "Next, I saw three men who each bore a barbed staff, and could run as swiftly as hares.

"Then I saw by the fire at the front of the hostel, a man with one eye, one hand, and one foot, and he had a squealing pig. Explain this."

"This," said Fer Rogain, "is the man with his pig who has brought doom to Conare this night, for his presence is geiss to the king."

Then Ingcél continued his account: "Next, I saw an apartment with twenty-seven men wearing black capes with white hoods and a red crest, and an iron brooch.

"Then I saw three fools by the fire. Such was the power of their humor that if any man in Ireland had the corpses of their parents laid at his feet, he could not help but laugh at the antics of these three.

"Then I saw an apartment with three men, each of whom had a cup of water with watercress in the water.

"Then I saw a man, blind in one eye, carrying a pig's head that was squealing. Explain that."

"This," said Fer Rogain, "is a swineherd

who always sheds blood wherever he feasts."

"Grief to him who proceeds with this destruction!" cried Lomnae Drúth.

"You do not rule here," warned Ingcél. "Bloody clouds engulf you!

"Arise! Plunderers, to the hostel!"

The Plunderers Are Routed

~

"Quiet," hushed Conare. "What is that noise?"

His friend Conall Cernach reported back that a war band of plunderers had encircled the building, and that their defenders were mobilizing.

Lomnae Drúth was the first to attack the entrance, and his head was severed from his body at once. His companions seized it and hurled it into the hostel, and three times it was thrown in and out of the hostel.

Three times the plunderers sought to set the hostel on fire, and three times the flames were doused.

Conare slew six hundred of the plunderers before he gathered his weapons, and fully as many afterward. And the plunderers of Britain and Ireland were routed.

But the druids who accompanied the plunderers remembered what Fer Rogain had said, and wrought spells to instill and increase such a thirst in Conare that he was forced to call for drink.

Macc Cécht, his mighty champion, was the one to whom Conare turned in his need. Macc Cécht answered that he would save his king from spears, but that the king had cupbearers to serve his drink.

When Conare had sought them out they told him that all the liquid in the hostel had been spent on dousing the several fires.

Again Conare turned to his champion for help, saying that protection from spears would not help if he were already dead from thirst.

The Death of Conare

~

At length Macc Cécht agreed to fetch water
for his king, and he fought his way out of the
hostel and through the marauding band. But
the enemy druids hid all the water in all the
lakes of Ireland, and even the rivers hid their
waters from him. Only Úarán Garaid did
not hide, and there he filled Conare's cup,
which was large enough to boil an ox.

But when he returned to the hostel the
following morning, Macc Cécht, in horror,
saw two men sever Conare's head from his
body.

One he decapitated, but the other took up
Conare's head as a trophy. Macc Cécht
heaved up a pillar and hurled it at the
running plunderer. It smote him deftly,
breaking his spine, then Macc Cécht struck
off his head.

Having recovered the head of Conare,

Macc Cécht carefully poured the draught of cool water into the gaping mouth.

When the cup was empty the severed head spoke for all to hear in praise of Macc Cécht's loyalty and kindliness.

Then it fell silent.

The Fates of Conare's Champion and Friend

By the close of the third day of combat fully four fifths of the plunderers had been slain.

Macc Cécht too, the king's champion, lay dying on the field of battle. A scavenging wolf was gnawing at his broken body, and he called to a woman nearby to tell him whether it was a fly, a midge or an ant that was on him. When she told him of the wolf he swore he had thought it merely the itching of a fly.

Then he died.

Conall Cernach, the king's truest friend, had left the field of battle alive.

When he returned to his home his father greeted him with disdain when he heard that he had not given his life in defense of the king, for it was a matter of bitter shame to flee and escape from the battle while the king had not.

Conall answered by showing him the wounds that he had suffered in his efforts to protect the king, his friend.

He had suffered one hundred and fifty wounds to his hand and arm that held his shield – these terrible gashes made by spears that had pierced his shield.

His other hand, that had engaged the enemy and dealt maiming and death with every blow of this weapon, was so slashed and gouged that the sinews barely held it together.

At the sight of these trophies his father welcomed his son home as a brave and seasoned warrior.

"Truly," he said, "you have served the drinks of death to many at Da Derga's hostel!"

TAMLANE AND THE
FAERY QUEEN

~

Few folk travel to the land of Faery, and fewer still ever return home. Yet for all its wonder and magic, Faeryland holds deadly perils for mortals who will not bend to its subtle laws.

Tamlane was the son of a laird living in Selkirkshire (now the Borders), Scotland. He had been taught the art of riding from an early age, and was accomplished in many arts besides, as befits the heir to a good estate.

When he was a child just nine years old, his uncle invited him to accompany him on a hunt with hawk and hounds. Although the Autumn clouds loomed dark with threats of storm, his young heart beat bravely as he rode forth with the company of hunters.

The further they rode, the higher grew the wind that blew from the realms of ice beyond the sea, and bitter was the journey. At length the gale began to howl through the treetops as loud as any man can shout, and a freezing rain began to lash the ill-fated company.

It tasked the men of all their strength to ride those long dark hours, but the child began to fall behind and was soon lost in the forest of Carterhaugh.

The Abduction

~

The Queen of Faery roamed with joy through the squall as it grew to a blizzard, and when she saw the child Tamlane her heart was moved with care.

Tamlane slept in his saddle with the warm, numb slumber that is the bitter-sweet refuge of folk freezing to death.

In her mantle of green the Faery Queen swept him off the stumbling horse which, with a resounding slap, she swiftly sent home to its stable. The child, though, she held in her arms and she spoke soothing words to rouse his spirit.

The instant he opened his eyes she succumbed to his innocent charms, and she bore Tamlane away to her court under the hill.

A Daring Maid

~

For fully six long years no one in Tamlane's family or friends knew anything except that he had been swallowed by the snowstorm. Yet fireside rumors haunted their minds when dark evenings grew long into Autumn.

Tales were told of a ghost that was not quite a ghost, and that stalked through the forest of Carterhaugh. "Tamlane" the rustic folk called the specter, though they rarely gave voice to their thoughts. When words were spoken though, then they muttered darkly of ancient magic and deeds that were not wholly of the mortal man's world.

Even at May Day, when the greenwood revels were gaily celebrated in every community, the forest of Carterhaugh stood somber and silent, for folks feared to tread in its shadows that seemed unnaturally dark and cold.

But one maid, the daughter of a local lord, for whom the forest formed part of her dowry, determined to see for herself what strange magic lurked in its clandestine heart.

On the eve of May Day while the sun was yet soaring the sky, she made her fateful decision. She dropped her needle to the floor, and let her silken embroidery fall to the chair as she scurried to the mirror to preen herself.

Her long yellow hair she braided above her brow, and fixed it with a comb of gold, then she tucked up her warm green skirt, and secretly left the house.

Deep in the forest is a glade with a well where a rose tree bears red blooms, and there she sat as the sunset flared red and pink through the branches. And there she plucked the sweetest rose flower with the darkest crimson hue. And there she snagged her finger on the bush's thorny stem, reddening its cruel curved tip.

Her gasp set the bird of silence to wing, and under its velvet shadow not a sound was uttered and not a creature stirred. Over all the forest a deep hush fell, and the lass gazed about through a mist of fear at the glade that now seemed so strange . . .

The Courtship of Tamlane

~

"Why?"

The sad man's softly spoken word came from behind her. She turned as swiftly as she could, but saw no one there.

"Why have you plucked the bloom from the bush?"

The voice was in front of her this time, and when she spun around she saw its source. The man was as gentle a man as ever walked the Earth, and there was none she knew of that could have been more handsome.

"I have this forest held in trust as my dowry come the day of my marriage. I have rights here. But who are you?"

Her dignity brightened his mind, and her beauty fired his heart.

"First they called me Jack, but never to my face; then they called me John, but only when they thought me gone; but Tamlane is the name my mother gave me, and you may call me that too."

There, as the dusk grew deeper around them, and the magical hush melted into the natural sounds of twilight, they discovered their love for each other, and lay down together. The mossy sward was their bed, the bole of an aged oak their pillow, and the peeping stars their coverlet.

The Pact Against the Faery Powers

~

With her arms laden with fragrant red roses, and a heart glowing with joy, the lass returned to her home.

But on that old bush by the well in the glade, they had found another rose that they'd left well alone. It was the tiny bud of a green-petaled flower that nestled in the protective ring of a spear-guard of doughty thorns . . .

This bud was the token of the unborn babe their love had conceived.

In urgent council then, they'd formed a bold plan to protect them all against Tamlane's jealous captor, the proud Queen of Faery.

The Fateful Night of Halloween

As the sun set and Halloween began, the lass faithfully followed Tamlane's advice, and scooped up a jar of the cold, clear water from the place where two gurgling streams meet.

She had anxiously awaited this special night for half a year, because now was the time to perform a desperate task she had vowed to perform, both for her own sake and for that of her unborn child.

On every Halloween the Faery Folk, in splendid panoply, ride forth from their underhill kingdom to celebrate Samhain, the ancient New Year. Once out, they swarm far and wide over all the land, and common folk stay home by the hearth, and bar their doors, and woe betide the wayfarer who rashly crosses their path!

On this one night Tamlane could leave the covert realm of the Faery Queen, albeit mounted on a spectral horse and riding with the Faery host. It meant that the mortal lass could once again see her true love.

However, if Tamlane was still with the court when dawn colored the sky and they returned to their wondrous realm, then he would have lived in Faeryland for a full seven years, and he would be doomed to remain there for evermore.

If her devotion couldn't capture him tonight, then the Faery Queen could claim his soul for all time!

The Faery Troop Ride By

~

By midnight she had hurried to Miles Cross and sprinkled the water, glittering in the white moonlight, in a broad circle all around her.

She did not wait long, huddled in her dark green mantle, before the unearthly company rode into view.

The first host rode horses as black as the sky between the stars, and she hid her face as they passed.

The second host rode horses as brown as the earth the fleshworm burrows, and she made many signs of reverent salute as the solemn host rode past.

The third host were mounted on steeds as white as the first snows of winter, and at the fore, with green cloaks fluttering, rode the Queen of Faery with Tamlane by her side. Upon his brow shone a golden star, a token of his mortal birth.

As his horse drew up in front of her she leaped and grabbed its bridle, and then tugged down the dream-eyed man on its back into the middle of the magic circle she'd cast.

A howl like the screeching of November owls all loosed upon the instant tore from the throat of the Queen.

But the woman held fast to her man . . .

The Transformations of Tamlane

~

Although no Faery wight could cross her circle, nothing prevented the Queen's own magic from affecting her erstwhile subject.

The young woman in love knew what was coming, and had been preparing herself for half a year, but the shock — when it came — nearly broke her resolve, and that would have shattered her heart.

The man face down on the bare earth beneath her began to melt away, and in his place arose a vast serpent. Squatting astride its writhing mass her hands all but slipped from its shuddering scales.

But she held on to her man lest her valiant heart break.

Amid a torrent of bitter curses, the Queen again wove her magic and the serpent dissolved into a newt that squirmed and heaved itself toward the circle's edge.

But she held on to her man, and brought him back from the brink.

Amid a hail of oaths, the Queen's spells turned Tamlane into a burning bale with clouds of sparks like viper's teeth spitting burning venom, and a bed of embers that could melt a rod of iron.

But she held on to her man, such was the blazing heat of the love in her heart.

Between teeth clenched like a mesh of icicles, the Faery Queen gave vent to her hatred and transfigured Tamlane into a dove whose every instinct was to soar into the heavens.

But she held on to her man: she was not deluded but knew that the Faery archers would loose their deadly barbs as soon as they left the circle.

With eyes of smoking darkness, the Queen gave the lass another reason to abandon her claim on Tamlane. Into the form of a sharp beaked swan whose neck could pierce any defense she turned him, and gloated as his powerful wings sought to beat off the woman that clung to him still.

But she held on to her man, ignoring the wounds and gashes that he heaped upon her bloodied body.

The Queen's Ultimate Weapon
~

A shudder of certain victory thrilled the Faery Queen as she remembered the shape of the creature that must ultimately conquer Tamlane's tenacious lover.

With a shriek of joy that was worse than her howl of anguish, the Queen wrought her magical transformation one more time.

The battling swan dissolved beneath the struggling and battered woman. In its place rose a powerfully built and implacable man.

Though naked as the day of his birth, his lack of metal weapons mattered not a bit – with his bare hands alone this vigorous man could tear her body apart!

The Dawning of Day

~

With a twist as quick as a hounded hare's, Tamlane's lover leaped from the back of her spell-bound man.

With practiced fingers she loosed the clasp that held her mantle around her shoulders, and before he could jump to his feet she swirled the cloak above her head.

As it rippled through the air her heart missed a beat and she stood on the threshold of doom.

With infinite slowness it settled down as the angry man rose to his feet.

As soon as it touched him Tamlane started melting again. Not in form this time, but in temper, and he grew less aggressive.

As it enveloped him more, the Queen's spell was further softened, and he felt his heart beat for the first time in seven years.

As he wrapped it around himself, scenting

his lover's perfume, the final bonds between him and the Queen were utterly and irreversibly broken.

His heart was free of Faery glamor, and the long dream of Faeryland finished.

"Had I known," hissed the Queen astride her white horse, "that you'd ever seen this wench, Tamlane, I'd have plucked out your eyes and given you orbs of yew.

"And had I known that your heart was given to this woman, I'd have ripped its flesh out of your body and given you a heart of granite!"

But though they stood only yards away, in their circle the couple were out of her reach.

And though the dawn was hours away, the Faery riders had far to go before they could return to their court under the hill.

Terrible the wails that rent the sky as the riders flew through that haunted Halloween night, and fearful the fate of any unprepared soul that they found wandering lost and alone and in peril.

Safe in their circle the lovers embraced for an hour, and then tended the wounds that she had sustained.

Bathed in the rosy light of dawn, Tamlane and his bride-to-be paced the now deserted road and entered the gloom of Carterhaugh forest, where they sought the rose by the well in the glade where they'd met.

The sun's first rays lit on the special green bud, the couple watched anxiously. At the touch of this light the bud slowly opened its unearthly green petals to its warmth.

As the petals drank the sunlight the bloom fully unfurled, eerie, almost menacing in its unearthly hue. But as they watched the color faded into gray, and then into the darkest red.

In another moment it shone with the brightest and most vibrant red of any that ever grew in the greenwood, and the unnatural shadows that had long plagued the forest dissolved like thawing snow, never to return.

All taint of Faery had been lifted from Tamlane, from Carterhaugh forest, and from the child that snuggled in the womb of the woman he loved!

TRUE THOMAS, THE RHYMER

~

The glamor of Faeryland can be very alluring, and many a simple man has been seduced by beautiful elf maidens into leaving his mortal life behind and voyaging to the magical realms of Faery – never again to be seen by his family and friends.

Sometimes, though, a man's love of his homeland can win against the Faery wiles, and enable him to return – at least for a while . . .

Thomas, the laird of Erceldoune, was a young man whose spirit was still free of the weight of duty that can bow the head with fatigue, turning it away from the dreaming contemplation of the naked sky – and he keenly enjoyed such simple pleasures!

May Day dawned brightly and the sun shone warmly where Thomas lay alone on the grass of Huntlie Bank. Thrushes and blackbirds sang the praises of the new day from the woodland nearby, and the air was filled with the sweet scents and the busy hum of Spring.

Above him, as he basked in the morning sunlight, stretched the canopy of an ancient rowan. It did not seem strange when a bird of colorful plumage flew up out of the east to perch awhile in the ample branches overhead.

With its bright bar of blue feathers no one could mistake it for anything but a jay, but there was an unusual softness in its cry as it loudly announced its presence to the world.

Thomas did sit up and take notice, however, when he saw a rider approaching from the same point as the jay. The bird called once more and commenced a slow and purposeful flight toward the Eildon tree where it settled and called again.

It struck Thomas that the rider was also traveling toward the Eildon tree. Mounted on a dappled gray palfrey rode a woman whose gleaming green silk clothes shone with embroidered gold and jewelry of bright oriental gems.

As she drew closer he saw that her forehead, framed by long tresses of coal-black hair, was as white as a swan. Her horse, royally saddled with glowing ivory, was also richly attired with precious stones. All the buckles were of beryl, the stirrups were of crystal, and mother-of-pearl shimmered on every strap, and the bridle itself was of glistening gold, and from it, on each side, hung three golden bells.

Seven greyhounds walked beside her, and seven scent-hounds also. Around her neck hung a horn of curious workmanship, and under her belt the huntress carried a full complement of arrows.

Not all the words in all the tongues of Earth could tell the full extent of her beauty, and Thomas determined that he must speak with her or die!

The Queen of Faeryland

~

With the speed and grace of a hart, Thomas leaped to his feet and bounded across the bonny meadow to the Eildon tree.

As she drew near he sank to his knee and addressed her with reverence.

"Lovely lady, have mercy on me, for you are surely the Queen of Heaven."

She replied with a voice as sweet as honey.

"Thomas, you are mistaken, for I am no Queen of Heaven, but a lady from another fair country. I am here to hunt the wild deer."

"If you would hunt then consider this, that I am captivated by your beauty, and though it would cost me my life I desire to lie with you."

"Well, Thomas, that would be folly. Surely once we had lain together the attraction of my beauty would fade in your eyes, and I would appear even less than commonplace."

"Lovely lady, look kindly on me and I swear I will love you constantly, and never stray from your side whether you choose to journey to heaven or even to hell."

There in the morning sunlight beneath the Eildon tree, the lady slipped off her mount and took the young man's hand. And, if ever any truth lies in legend, we must believe they lay together fully seven times!

The Transformation of the Queen

~

With mixed emotions, the Queen protested that she was exhausted by their lovemaking, and swore that no woman ever born could outdistance him in this sport!

Thomas stood and stared over the valley as proudly as any stag, then turned to gaze upon his beloved.

His heart forgot to beat for a space.

Her glossy black hair had turned to the color of ashes, and her glorious clothes were tattered and pale. Her eyes, that had flashed with passion's bright fire, were now gray and clouded, and her soft, almost translucent, skin was now like lead sheeting.

"Grief!" he cried. "So faded is the face that once outshone the sun!"

"Bid goodbye," said the wizened Queen in a rising voice, "to sun and moon, and farewell to blade of grass and leaf of tree. For you must come away with me to where no sight of Middle Earth can be seen!"

Thomas stared again, in stark sorrow now, at the valley and the vista before him. He knew full well that he might never see his homeland again, and wondered in what distant place his bones would be laid to rest.

But his oath was his bond, and his future now lay with the wizened hag who rose up before him, offering him her bony hand.

She led him deftly along an invisible path through a dense thicket maze. The scent of the countless white blossoms, covering the boughs like drifts of perfumed snow, was intoxicating and nearly overpowered his mind. With unerring care though, Thomas took pains to step directly in the footprints of the fleetly moving Queen, for the vicious thorns that lurked beneath the blooms could rend a suit of studded leather!

At length they broke from cover into a

glade of warmth and dappled sunlight. There lay the secret entrance to a gloomy cave into whose cold mouth Thomas walked with a heavy heart – but never a backward glance.

The Orchard of Surfeit

~

Deep into Eildon Hill Thomas traveled with the Queen.

For three days and nights they walked in midnight blackness, through a chilling liquid that rose to the knee. And all along Thomas heard nothing but the incessant roar of distant cataracts and waterfalls.

Just when Thomas felt that hunger must make his steps falter and he would stumble and perish in the sweeping current, he saw light ahead, and his strength rallied.

The cave opened into a cavern of unguessable dimensions, and there Thomas saw a vast garden with orchards of pears, apples, damsons, figs, grapes and dates.

All the trees were heavy with fruit, and through their boughs flew countless colorful birds. The air was thick with their enchanting song and above it all rose the peerless melody of the nightingale.

Although dazzled by the beauty of the subterranean bower, Thomas was still gnawed by hunger, and he reached up to pluck an apple that shone with all the hues of the airy pyre of sunset.

"Hold your hand!" cried the Queen. "Let the apple go. To taste the fruits here quenches mortal hunger so fully that anyone who eats of its tempting bounty will never again feel the pangs of appetite.

"Death devours anyone who seeks to fill their stomach here!"

The Journey to Faeryland

~

"Come to me, Thomas." The Queen spoke with a captivating gentleness in her voice as she sat on the soft grass. "Lay your head in my lap."

Relieved by her heartwarming tone, grateful for the chance of a rest, and moved above all by his abiding devotion to her, Thomas gladly did as he was invited.

"Here you will see," she continued as he nestled down, "a more marvelous sight than any of your countrymen ever saw.

"Look up now and see the mountain where peace and plenty are but the gateway to the heaven that awaits the mindful pilgrim.

"Look down now and see the valley path that leads to the rare delights of the eternal realm of paradise.

"Look now across the broad open plain

where roam the multitude who waste their time in fruitless quests.

"Look down again, and further down now to see the cliff over which many fall to enter the dark vent that leads to eternal darkness.

"Look again close by, and you will see the modest hill where resides all the glorious mystery of Faeryland. Atop this hill rises the undying castle whose beauty is famed further than any mortal realm, and whose treasures are unmatched by any dreams of wealth that occupy the minds of Middle Earth.

"That is the castle where I hold sovereign sway."

Welcome to Faeryland

~

As soon as Thomas saw the hill with the marvelous castle he made to move toward it – and when he turned to look into the face of the Queen his heart flooded with joy, and his sight swam with wonder as if veils of cloud were parting to reveal the radiant, star-crowned moon!

There she was, robed with gleaming green silk, and mounted on her dappled palfrey, with twice-seven hounds that stood alert and loyal all around her.

She had regained all the beauty that had been hers when first they'd met.

"Words," she said with a note of severity in her voice, "wield magic in Faeryland. You must take care of your eager tongue, and ensure you speak to no one at all but me."

With this warning she turned toward the

castle, put her horn to her lips and sounded a note that was clear and shrill, arcing like a rainbow to the topmost tower.

In a moment a glimmering tide, sparkling brightly with all the colors of the summer flowers, swept out of the main gate and poured toward them. These were the elves of her court, all dressed in costumes of green but bedecked with dazzling jewels in honor of their Queen's arrival home.

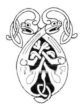

Sojourn in Faeryland

~

All manner of sweet and nourishing foods, along with delicious and refreshing drinks, were brought to them by the welcoming elves.

Thomas was given a high-stepping horse to ride into the crystal city, and amid the fanfare and joyous commotion, he felt more regal than any mortal king.

Despite the intoxication of the revels with which they were greeted once they had entered through the prodigious gateway, Thomas was ever wary of the destructive power of even one unguarded word, and faithfully directed all the passions of his heart and mind toward his Queen alone.

This was well done, for a single word could shatter the bright trust they shared, and ensnare his spirit in the dark sleep that steals upon folks cursed with forgetfulness.

For the penalty of breaking this lore of Faeryland is to be instantly exiled back to Middle Earth, never to be able to forget the magic and beauty of the castle on the hill, but be haunted endlessly by its undying memory!

For now, though, Thomas enjoyed all the delights of Faeryland.

Their days were spent in riding together through the wonderful countryside around the hill, and their evenings were spent in feasting, dance and song, and their nights were always spent together.

Lacking no stimulating entertainment for their complete satisfaction, and with no troubles to mar their perfect happiness, Thomas and the Queen of Faeryland enjoyed the full unfurling of their blossoming love . . .

The Way Home

~

Such was the pace of their carousing, and their deep involvement in each other, that the days all blurred together in a vision of joy unbounded, and the nights grew seamlessly into one long dream of bliss.

When a day came, therefore, that as they strolled through that verdant land, the Queen asked Thomas how long he had dwelt with her in the castle of Faery, he answered: "Why, just a few days, surely no more than three?"

"Thomas . . ." she replied sadly, "it is fully seven years — a blink to the eye of eternity but long enough for a child to become a man.

"If you were to stay here another night then your soul would be bound here for all time."

"Such is the future I desire!"

"But before I allow you to take this great

step, I must be sure of the depth of your love."

"Surely there is no question . . ?"

"None that we may ask here. But if you were to return to your homeland, perhaps you would find yourself disenchanted of our Faery world, and seek again the pleasures of Middle Earth, those natural pleasures of the life you had yet to live."

"I protest!"

"You have loved me well and truly, and I shall not strip from you this final chance to live your Earthly life among your kith and kin."

With a wave of her milk-white hand the realm of Faery dissolved like snow in the dawn of spring, and in its place he saw the old familiar site of Huntlie Bank.

They stood and embraced under the spreading branches of the Eildon tree, then she leaped upon her palfrey and took her horn in her hand.

"Wait one moment!" cried Thomas in anguish. "If I am to be imprisoned here in Middle Earth to prove my love for you, at least give me the comfort of some token of your love for me."

"You will be master of the harp, and be possessed of a tongue that charms the wise and witless equally. Moreover you will be able to answer every question with the truth."

"Will I never see you again?"

"One day, perhaps, you'll come for me, and we will meet again standing in the dappled light beneath the Eildon tree . . ."

A Singular Visitor

~

Although his estate had been well maintained in the seven years since he'd left, the seven years that followed his return saw its prosperity soar beyond all bounds.

His prowess as a bard was peerless, and he was welcomed in every home; his wisdom was beyond all measure, and he was courted by kings; his gifts extended into prophesy, and his insight kept him and the kingdom around him safe from all harm.

But his heart never gave up the love of the Faery Queen, and through all those years of success and wealth, he never truly knew joy again.

In truth he pined for the rarer treasures and the unbridled wonders that were freely found everywhere in the castle on the hill.

It chanced that the festival of May Day, on the seventh year after his return, found him once again back in his own lands of Erceldoune.

As he sat at the head of the great hall, absorbed in the rites of Spring, a commotion arose at the door that engaged his attention at once.

With a slow, steady flight a colorful bird had entered, flying straight for True Thomas the Rhymer!

The Call

❧

The jay, for – recognizable by the bright flash of blue on its wings – such it surely was, wheeled and perched on the high back of Thomas' chair.

The company were amazed as Thomas arose and let it step tamely onto his arm like a hunting hawk.

It called out with, for a jay, an unusually soft voice. Its cry seemed to speak straight to the hearts of those who heard it, telling of half-remembered dreams of beauty and freedom.

Then, as the people stood transfixed, bewildered by the curious visions that still enchanted their minds, Thomas walked out of the hall . . .

The Reunion

~

When the attendants at the hall had recovered their senses, Thomas was nowhere to be seen.

He had taken nothing with him save the clothes he wore and the jay that perched like a hunting bird on his arm.

His serving men quickly sent for their horses and rode abroad seeking him. Far and wide they spread their search, heedless of the festivities that everywhere celebrated this special day of the year.

When they returned that evening to tell of the hunt, none had set eyes on either Thomas or the bird.

Nothing unusual at all had been seen, excepting only that one young rider told in glowing terms of a hind and a hart that he had seen nuzzling under Eildon tree.

"When I drew near," he said, with awe in

his voice, "they turned to face me before walking steadily away, one beside the other. And no matter how quickly I rode I could not draw any closer!

"At length I watched them enter an impenetrable thicket of the most glorious May blossom, and they disappeared behind its scented veil amidst a shower of fluttering white petals . . ."

The Legacy of True Thomas the Rhymer

~

Over the years, indeed, the centuries since Thomas went away, many people claim to have seen him.

Sometimes he leaves his new home, either by the entrance under Eildon Hill or by various others, to talk to and trade with the people he meets.

One such man had taken two fine stallions to market yet, unaccountably, had received only derisory offers when he tried to sell them.

Walking home in the moonlight over a particularly lonely stretch of the Eildon Hills, he met a stranger mantled in a dark green cloak, who offered him a handsome sum for the horses.

They struck the deal and the stranger invited the farmer to see his stables. Accepting, the farmer was led into the side of the hill, through a tunnel into a cavern where the stranger revealed himself as Thomas.

Here was a host of sleeping warriors, and on a table was a mighty sword and a rousing horn. Thomas said that whoever took up the sword and blew the horn would become king of Britain, but warned that it must be done in the correct sequence.

The farmer blew the horn to rouse the men and then tried to lift the sword, but he couldn't.

Thunder grew out of the echoes of the horn blast, and the farmer found himself suddenly out on the open hillside again. But in that thunder he heard a voice:

"Grief to the coward, that prating, false lord,

Who sounds the alarm before raising his own sword!"

The Ballad of Alison Gross

~

Oh Alison Gross, who lives in yon tower,
The ugliest witch in the north country,
Beguiled me one day up to her bower,
And many sweet words she said to me.

She stroked my head, and she combed my
    hair,
And she said, "If you'll be my lover true,
This robe of silk, this jewelled cup,
And many more fine things will I give to
    you . . ."

"Away, away you ugly witch!
Stay back, stay back, and let me be!
I never will be your lover true
And I wish I were far from your company!"

She spun around and around about,
And thrice she blew on a grass-green horn,
And she swore by the moon and the stars
above
She'd make me rue the day I was born.

From her apron she took a silver wand,
Spoke spells and spun her three times round,
And she turned me into an ugly worm,
Condemned to crawl upon the ground . . .

But it came about last Hallowe'en,
When the Faery Court was riding by,
The Queen lighted down on the heathery
bank
Not far from the place I was wont to lie.

She took me up in her milk-white hands,
And stroked me three times across her knee,
And turned me into my proper shape.
Damn the witch, and bless that fair Lady!

The Wife of Usher's Well

~

There lived a wife at Usher's Well,
And a wealthy wife was she;
She had two stout and stalwart sons,
And she sent them over the sea.

They hadnae been a week from her,
A week but barely three,
When word came to that aged wife
That her sons she'd ne'ermore see.

"I wish the wind may never cease
Nor flashes in the flood,
Til my twa sons come home to me
In earthly flesh and blood!"

The hallowed days of Yule were come,
Nights were dark and snow lay wan,
When in and came her ain two sons,
Their hats bound wi' slim birchen wands.

Birch frae nither forest glen
Nor any mountainside,
But frae the tree that grows hard by
The gates of Paradise.

"Stoke up the fire, my merry maidens,
Bring water from the well!
For all my house shall feast this night
Since my twa sons are well."

But when the cock crowed up the sun
And dawn's fair chorus called for day,
The elder to the younger said
"Brother, we must away.

"The cock does crow, the day does dawn,
The nibbling worm does chide,
And if we're missed out o' our place
In Hell we must abide!"

"But if we leave our mither now
I fear she'll die o' grief,
Oh long may it be ere we meet again
Though life be all too brief.

Fare ye well, my mither dear!
Farewell tae barn and byre!
And fare ye well, yon bonny lass
That kindles now the cosy fire!"